HE RESCUED ME

HE RESCUED ME

FROM BEING HEARTBROKEN TO FINDING LOVE

TYLER MATTHEW GEBHARDT

TG Creatives LLC

Psalm 18:16

"He reached down from Heaven and Rescued me; he drew me out of deep waters."

This book is dedicated to my grandfather, Donald. His enormous influence on my life displays today, even after passing away in my early twenties. His love that he had for his family and the Lord showed me how genuinely selfless he was.

I love and miss you, Grandpa.

I have tried to recreate events, locales, and conversations from my memories of them. In order to maintain their anonymity, in some instances, I have changed the names of individuals and places, I may have changed some identifying characteristics and details such as physical properties, occupations, and areas of residence.

CONTENTS

CONTENTS

This book was written because I wanted to share how I found love in a dark place. You frequently hear about people who are at rock bottom, like former inmates, drug addicts, and gang members finding Jesus.

I found Jesus, or He found me, when I was heartbroken. Everyone could have a different rock bottom; mine happened because of a broken heart.

This book takes place in my mid to late twenties over four years. From fear and depression to hope and love, this book takes you through my journey and how God knew what He was doing the entire time.

My prayer is that this book helps you understand who God really is. I hope, from these pages, you can find the insight to get a better understanding of what true love is. May these pages bring you closer to Jesus and show you why we need Him in our lives.

In Jesus' name, Amen.

*This book is not a substitution for the Bible. The purpose of this book is to lead you in that direction.

INTRODUCTION

I used to frequently sit near our neighborhood water tower on a hill that overlooked the city in the far distance. The water tower had been tagged with the phrase, "Save the bees" in small letters towards the top. Several blue spruce pine trees would give me shade by a giant rock I would sit on. You could see for miles and it was peaceful for being in the suburbs.

All the times I have gone, I never once saw anybody else there sitting on my rock. It wasn't difficult to get to and I know people would find it to be breathtaking, but they still wouldn't go. I guess you could say that that rock under the blue spruce pine tree by the water tower was mine.

I would stay there for about an hour or until my body was getting sore from sitting on the, not so comfortable, rock. I'd pray and talk to God the entire time, mostly about how I was desperate for Him to change my life. To bring me to where I needed to go, so I could have the blessings I had been praying for, for years. I tried to get these blessings on my own and every time I would fail. It brought me to a dark place where I was depressed and had anxieties I couldn't shake. I was desperate for God and for change.

I always felt a feeling of peace on that rock by the water tower because I felt closer to God. It was just Him and me with no other distractions from the world. It was a way for me to focus on God and tell Him what was on my mind. I know He always listened to me because He cared for me. It was the reassurance of the peace He gave me when I was talking to Him on that rock. It was my refuge.

Growing up, I never had that rock by a water tower sanctuary to frequently go to whenever I needed to be alone to recharge my batteries. I never prayed or talked to God either. I didn't understand who God was and didn't have any desire to pursue Him. I believed in Jesus, but that was just because that is what I was taught. To me, Jesus was someone you had to believe in because being an atheist meant going to hell. Being an atheist meant you were the bad guy in a superhero movie. I didn't want that, so I believed in Jesus, but didn't know anything about Him.

I grew up in a Christian household where we just went through the motions of what we thought Christians should do. We weren't Bible thumpers or front-row pew participants, but we thought we were good people in general. We all tried to do the right thing, all the time. My parents set a great example by rarely drinking alcohol or even muttering a cuss word when I was growing up. They loved my siblings and me and loved each other wholeheartedly, which set the foundation for showing me what love was supposed to be. We went to church some Sunday mornings and celebrated Christian holidays. We even prayed as a family before dinner we had together to give thanks to God.

"Bless us, Oh Lord,
and these thy gifts which

we are about to receive from thy bounty,
through Christ, Our Lord.
Amen."

Nevertheless, I didn't understand who Jesus was or cared to. I was told that He loved us and that He saved us from our sins by dying on the cross. But I didn't fully grasp it or understand it. This is just what I was told growing up, so I went along with it. The Bible seemed confusing and scary to me, so I never decided to open it. I couldn't care less about deepening my faith and pursuing Christ because my mind was on other ventures.

I was engrossed in finding true love. I wanted a wife one day more than anything and wouldn't stop for anyone or anything. To be married with children seemed appealing to me. I saw what my parents had and wanted that for myself. I wanted to be married to my best friend and raise a beautiful family together. I wanted the American Dream and would stop at nothing to get it. I just needed to find the girl and everything else would come along with her.

I went out into this crazy, but beautiful world looking for love on my own. I was going to be someone's prince charming and they were going to be my beautiful princess. My love life was going to be the next Disney movie and everyone was going to be jealous of what I had. My love life was going to be the standard for what people wanted in their lives. I was one hundred percent certain it would happen because all I needed to do was find the one girl that was meant for me.

I tried for years and years just to be disappointed time and time again. I thought I found love a couple of different times but was foolishly mistaken. Either, the girl didn't turn out to be who I thought she was, or I was inexperienced and would ruin the re-lationship before it even started. Dating in the twenty-first century was more challenging than I had thought. You would think that it should be easy because everyone was just a swipe away, but that was the problem. There are too many options for people in the dating world today and living in a hook-up culture makes it difficult to find someone worthwhile. It was like shopping at a thrift store trying to find that rare item. I went into depression and was convinced that love was never going to happen in my life.

I would eventually find love, but it wasn't what I thought it was going to be. It is the greatest love I have or will ever experience in my life. It came at a time when I needed it the most and I am beyond grateful for it. This love changed my life for the better and saved me from myself. I was lost in this world with nowhere to go until this love found me. It was the love I was searching for when I first set out on my conquest to find it but would fail countless times. This is a love that you can find for yourself too; you have to have faith in it.

1

I Wanted Love

John 15:13

"Greater love has no one than this: to lay down one's life for one's friends."

What I wanted growing up was to find love. To find that special someone to spend the rest of my life with. I wanted her to be my best friend and would we do everything together. I wanted us to be in a fairy tale marriage where everyone was envious of what we had. I wanted, what I thought was, picture-perfect love. I wanted to love and be loved and wasn't going to stop until I got it.

But what exactly was love? I defined love as an intense feeling of deep affection for someone or an excessive interest and pleasure in something. To be invested in someone or something that you would do anything in your power to have it. Love seemed to have a straight-forward definition that anyone could define easily.

In high school, my favorite television show was "The Office." Jim and Pam were a great example of what I thought love was. Jim pursued Pam for years and built a great foundation with her on friendship. They would be seen laughing and spending a lot of the

| 1 |

scenes in the show together, they were inseparable. But Pam was engaged to another man and whenever he was around, Jim would slide away into the background or find something else to occupy his time with. He eventually tried to kiss her and she complied, but would later regret it. Jim couldn't take it anymore that the girl he loved was engaged to another man, so he decided to transfer to another branch. Pam would eventually call off her engagement months later and begin to realize how much she missed Jim. Jim started dating another girl from the other branch and his love life seemed to be going well. Until his branch had to merge with his old branch where Pam was because the company was downsizing. Jim was right back to the branch he had just left months ago to get away from the girl he couldn't have. Eventually, Pam would share her feelings for Jim, but he was dating someone else. Over the next couple of episodes, Pam seemed to be moving on and happy for the couple. Then, out of nowhere, Jim asks Pam out to dinner and the rest is history.

I saw what my parents had and wanted that for myself. They both worked at Target where they met each other in their late teenage and early adult years. My dad pursued my mom, but she kept turning him down until she eventually gave him a shot. They would go on to start dating and the rest is history. They were instrumental in my passion for finding a spouse so that I could be like them. They had a beautiful, loving family that did everything together. My dad would coach our little league sports and my mom would be at every game we had cheering us on. We went on vacations together to Disney Land, Camp Snoopy at the Mall of America, and several beaches across the United States. My childhood was excellent and I wanted a family one day to love like I was loved. To say I am genuinely grateful for my upbringing would be an understatement.

My grandfather, Donald, was also a significant component in why I was so passionate about finding a spouse. I never met his wife,

Louise, because she died before I was born, but he loved her so much that he never dated anyone after her. He knew that she was the one and that she was waiting for him in Heaven. It always brought a tear to my eye because I thought it was one of the most romantic things I have ever heard. He would go on to live without dating anyone for the next twenty-five years until he eventually passed away.

I didn't have much luck dating in high school and college. I was super shy and it took me a couple of months to get comfortable in front of people. I didn't have my first girlfriend until I was a senior in high school. I thought she was attractive but was not the typical girl I would see myself dating. She cussed like a sailor, smoked weed, and had nothing in common with me. We never talked about it while we were dating, but I know she wasn't a believer. At the time, I didn't care. I was desperate to get a girlfriend for the first time, so I went along with it, I was trying to find love.

She made all the first moves, from liking my photos on social media to talking to my friends about me. I never had a girl that I found to be pretty and that they found me attractive like that before. I was in a new territory and it felt good to be sought after by someone. Even if us together didn't make any logical sense.

We didn't date for very long and I didn't have that feeling of love pouring from my heart at any time during our relationship. The truth is, we didn't have anything in common and it wasn't the love I was looking for. I ended up breaking up with her and never talked to her again. I have no idea what she is up to now, but I pray that she is doing well.

I dated another girl in high school and the same thing happened where I didn't pursue them first and they did all the work. I found her attractive, so I went along with it. I was seeking the title of having a girlfriend to have credibility with my classmates instead of staying single and dating the right girl for me.

I blame my immature attitude, inexperience, and trying to elevate my popularity status. I was young and naive but didn't care or know better. It did feel good to be wanted, but it was unfair to them because I never liked those girls in the first place.

There were always a couple of girls I would have my heart set on during my high school days, but would never ask them out or tell them I liked them because I was afraid of rejection and the embarrassment of everyone else knowing. I had confidence issues and was still trying to find myself. It wasn't until my late twenties to where I would discover whom I needed to be.

Searching For Love

Proverbs 18:22
"He who finds a wife finds what is good and
receives favor from the Lord."

When I started getting out into the dating world in my twenties, I was newer to the dating game and never pursued anyone before. My high school dating career can be summed up easily, non-existent. The girls I did date in the past pursued me and I just went along with it. I had zero experience of pursuing a girl and being the one to initiate it. All I know is, that I wanted to find my soulmate with all of my heart and I wanted to see her soon. I still had dreams of finding the perfect girl for me, so I decided to start looking for her.

I went to a university in downtown Denver, Colorado where it was a commuter college and nobody lived on or near campus. Nonetheless, there were a lot of attractive, intelligent, driven girls that went there and I had a lot of them in my classes. I even got the courage to start conversations with these girls, but that was because we would be partnered up in group projects. Nonetheless, I did start to get to know some of them.

There was this one girl named Jazmine that I would become pretty close with. I saw her two times a week and would look forward to it. She was beautiful and everything I would want in a potential spouse. We had great chemistry and didn't struggle to keep a conversation going.

It was her idea to study in person one late afternoon after class for our midterm test. This was going to be the most straightforward midterm test and I wasn't planning on studying for it, but I agreed because I had a crush on her and would get to see her outside of school.

We met at her place, which was only a couple minutes away from the university. It was downtown near 16th street mall and you could feel the atmosphere that came with it. It was dark outside and all the holiday lights were lit up.

Her roommates were gone, which was nice because then we could concentrate on studying and not be distracted by them. I sat down at the kitchen table, opened my backpack, and took out my book and notepad. She pushed a chair right up next to mine and sat down.

We began to study and she started acting different than usual. She was being super flirtatious and touched my leg frequently. She never did that before and it caught me off guard at first until I got more comfortable with her and started doing it back to her. I liked it because I barely got the chance to be close to a woman. She kept changing the subject from studying to how she wanted to go into her room and watch a movie. She was hinting at something and I didn't pick it up because of my inexperience with dating. At one time, she got closer to my face while staring at my lips and I didn't know why. Then, she pulled away. I rejected her and didn't even know it. She wanted me to kiss her. Again, did I say I lacked experience?

An hour later I decided I needed to go home to get to bed because I had class early the following day. I thought we had a great time together and couldn't wait to see her again in class in a few days. I had a crush on this girl and she seemed to be giving me attention. I thought it could potentially blossom into something.

The next time I saw her in class she was not her usual self. She was short with me and would avoid me at all costs. We used to sit next to each other, but this time sat on the other side of the room. After class, she bolted away before I could ask her if I did something wrong.

When I reflect on it, I rejected her attempt of her trying to kiss and sleep with me, which would bring her to move on to someone else. She wasn't trying to date anyone, so instead would "enjoy" her college life by having fun. She got the sense that I was looking for a serious relationship and that I was also inexperienced.

A couple of weeks later, I downloaded every dating application you could think of to my phone and started swiping on anyone I found attractive. It didn't matter to me if we had anything in common. I was naïve and didn't understand that for a relationship to work out in the long term, you would need some things in common.

I would get some matches a couple of times a week, message a couple of them and eventually go on dates. It was exciting at the start of this journey because I felt I had an endless pool of potential dates. It wasn't until later that I realized that very few people were taking dating seriously anymore and most wanted to sleep around. It was a shock for me because I thought everyone wanted what I wanted. Which was love and to be loved by your best friend.

After years of trying online dating, I came across a beautiful girl named Aly. She was a devoted Christian, which I thought was marvelous, but didn't know much about it. We hit it off immediately and would go on a couple of dates together. She eventually brought up her Christianity and how much she loved Jesus. She asked me, "Do you take your faith seriously?"

I said, "I believe in Jesus, but don't know much about Christianity." You could tell she wasn't sure how to respond to my answer. She thought for a couple of seconds and then said, "I want to wait for marriage to have sex, is that something you'd want to do?"

"I'm not sure that is something I want to do," I said knowing that she wasn't going to like my answer. She nodded and reached into her purse for her phone. She showed me a Bible Application that she used every day. I was intrigued by Jesus, so I downloaded it onto my phone. She set it up to where I would get a Bible verse sent to me every single day, which I still get to this day.

Looking back, I think she convinced herself that she could help me see Jesus as she saw Him. She was a year older than me and was losing patience with her love life. After getting to know me, she started to catch feelings and wanted us to blossom into something. She eventually brought up how she wanted to wait for marriage to have sex again to no avail. She drew a line in the sand and I had no desire to wait until marriage. So, we stopped seeing each other after that. I took it hard at first because I liked her. She too liked "The Office" and her personality reflected that.

Online dating was more complicated than I imagined it to be because initially, I thought with the dating pool at my fingertips, that one of them would eventually become mine. I wasn't about to give up because I wanted love more than anything, but it was starting to weigh on my heart.

3

My First Love

*"And now these three remain: faith, hope and love.
But the greatest of these is love."*

After college, I worked for a major airline at Denver International Airport. I did the payroll, scheduling, bookkeeping, and vacation for the aircraft mechanics. I had a lot of people come in and out of my office with scheduling problems, vacation requests, and payroll issues. The job itself wasn't the best, but it was somewhere where I could start a career and it gave me the grand prize of flying for free on standby.

After a couple of months, I eventually became relatively close with a lot of the aircraft mechanics. Most of them were the same age as my parents because the Denver station always had high seniority, so there was an age gap of about thirty years or so, but we got along incredibly. There was enjoyable banter among each other and I would look forward to going to work on Monday because of it.

I walked into my office one morning, put my lunch down, and started up my computer. While it was booting up, I went over to the coffee machine just outside of my office and poured a cup of coffee. I had a coffee mug that stated, "World's Best Boss." Just like the one Michael Scott had in the television show, "The Office." I drank my coffee strictly for the caffeine intake. I never added sugar or creamer to my coffee and enjoyed drinking it black. As my sister would often sarcastically say, "enjoy your hot bean water." A lot of guys would tease me at work too for my lack of taste when it came to coffee, but it was all in good fun.

As I got back into my office two coworkers were sitting down on the chairs across from my desk. Their names were Ed and John and I was close with both of them. I could tell right away that Ed was in my office for a purpose. They both greeted me and then Ed nervously asked, "Are you a Christian?"

I replied, "Yes, I am."

Then, they both got up and left. We often talked about my dating life, so he knew I was single, but I wasn't sure why he would be asking me that.

I thought to myself, "Maybe he wants me to join his church or something?" I wondered what that was all about for a couple of minutes and then went back to my work since my computer was finally booted up.

Roughly two to three weeks later, Ed and John walked into my office and sat down across from my desk again. This time Ed asked me "Can I give you my daughter's phone number?"

My initial reaction was somewhat along the lines of surprise, shock, and excitement. I looked over at John and he kind of smiled at me. I confusedly asked, "Does she know about you doing this?"

Ed laughed out loud and said, "Yes she does, I showed her a picture of you online and I talk about you all the time."

I asked him, "Can I see a picture of her?"

He then showed me this picture of her that wasn't the highest quality and she was in the distance. You could barely tell what she looked like.

I told him reluctantly, "I'll take her number."

Ed then gave me a sticky note with the name "Jennifer" and her number on it. I thanked him for giving me her number because I know many fathers wouldn't do that to just anyone. I was touched because he thought I was a good enough person to date his daughter. He then left the room with John as John turned around and smiled at me. He didn't say anything and then exited the room.

I ended up texting Jennifer later that day saying who I was and what her father, Ed did. I waited patiently throughout the afternoon and she didn't reply. I didn't think of it much since I hardly knew her or what she looked like. I ended up trying to find her on social media to get a better picture of her, but could never find her. She didn't reply until later that evening. She apologized and thought she replied earlier.

We texted back and forth getting to know each other for the next couple of days and I realized that we had a lot in common. I asked her on a date to a local 'pour it yourself' brewery. She said "yes" and was super excited to meet me since her father, Ed, talked about me all the time. We made the date for the following weekend.

We decided to wait for each other outside the brewery and then go inside together. I parked my truck in the parking lot and started walking toward the entrance. I was the first one there, so I sat on a bench near the front door and waited for her. I wasn't nervous sitting there waiting for her because to me it was just another date and I had no idea what she looked like.

After a couple of minutes, I saw Jennifer walk around the corner and I immediately felt the butterflies in my stomach. She was a gorgeous woman that seemed to be well put together. She dressed conservatively and had the most beautiful smile I have ever seen in my entire life. I don't know if it was love at first sight or not, but I was feeling the butterflies in my stomach and I was nervous now.

We both hugged each other and introduced ourselves. Then, we proceeded to the front door as I grab the handle and opened the door for her. She seemed impressed and with a big smile said "thank you!" As we walked in the door, I remember thinking how great her smile was. I was in love with her smile and thought it was the most beautiful smile in all of the world. We walked over to the hostess table and paid to get in. It was a 'pour it yourself' brewery where you walked up to the beer taps and picked out which beer or seltzer you wanted. We both picked out our beers and headed for an empty spot outside on the back balcony.

We started conversing and after a couple of minutes I asked her, "Has your dad ever set you up with someone before?"

She laughed out loud and said, "Absolutely not! You're definitely the first person."

I laughed and asked, "did you approve of your dad giving me your number?"

She laughed again and said, "I reluctantly gave him the approval because he didn't have a very good picture of you. He just thought highly of you, so I decided it was ok!"

I said, "The same thing happened to me! The picture that he had of you was out of focus and you were in the distance." We both laughed and picked on Ed for his lack of having good pictures of us.

We talked for a couple of hours and got to know each other. During the date, you could feel the connection that we had and I didn't want it to end. I've never been on a date before where the conversation came as easy as it did and we had a lot in common.

I ended up closing the tab and paying for the beers that we had. She thanked me for buying while she smiled at me and I could feel my heart beating faster. Jennifer's smile was my weakness. I walked her to her car and told her, "Text me when you get home, so I know you got there safely."

She smiled and said "Okay!"

I hugged her and started walking back to my truck. My mind was racing a hundred miles an hour. I was eager for what was to come with her and couldn't wait to see her again. I remember thinking on my drive home that God brought her into my life for a reason.

"Thank you, God, for bringing Jennifer into my life. I have no idea why you brought her into my life, but I'm glad you did." I said to myself while smiling with joy that I've never felt before.

She texted me when she got home and said that she had a great time and is looking forward to seeing me again. She thanked me for buying drinks and for walking her to her car. She wanted to see me again, but it would have to wait because she was going to be out of town the following week.

A couple of dates later, we went to dinner at a popular chain steak place. We met there after work one day and things were progressing well with Jennifer. She wanted to see me all the time and I was thoroughly enjoying her company. It was about this time when I was catching real feelings for her. I know it was only a couple weeks into seeing her, but I was naïve and didn't know better. In reality, I didn't know her that well and I was immature when it came to dating, but I wanted love more than anything.

Anyways, the date was going along as we were chatting, but you could tell something was different about her. She gave off the vibe that she was thinking about something else the whole time. Then, during the meal, she said, "I want to talk to you about something."

My heart sunk to my stomach as I was imagining the worst possible scenarios. "What could this be about," I thought to myself. I replied nervously, "What is it?"

She said, "I just wanted to say that I was dating this guy before you and that I was having a tough time getting over and that you have helped me in that process. But, I'm just not all the way over him yet, but I am close. I just don't want him to get in the way of what I think we can become."

I was shocked to hear this, but it didn't put a damper on things. She wanted to see where she and I could go and didn't want him to be in our way. "Thank you for being honest with me and communicating this. I know it could be hard to get over someone" I said. She seemed relieved by what I said and you could tell she was happy all of the sudden.

I said, "Look, I get that you still have feelings for this guy, and that is ok! I know breakups are tough and that it takes time to move on. We will just keep taking things like we are and see what happens!"

She seemed comforted as she said, "Thank you for understanding! I was scared you would be turned off and would have stopped seeing me. Thanks for understanding and being you!"

It was at this moment that our relationship started blossoming. We started getting closer and closer with each passing day. I was falling in love with the girl I wanted to spend the rest of my life with. She was everything I thought I wanted in a girl and she had a smile to die for. I have found what I thought was love. I couldn't wait for what the future held for the both of us.

4

My First Heartbreak

Psalm 34:18
"The Lord is close to the brokenhearted and saves
those who are crushed in spirit."

A couple of months have passed since Jennifer and I started dating and it wasn't as great as I thought it was going to be at this point. But I was still in love and was optimistic it could get better. She ended up getting a new job during this time that she was struggling to get accustomed to and hardly had as much time for me anymore. We still saw and talked to each other, but the frequency wasn't as high as it was when we first started dating. Which was okay because I knew she was stressed because of work and I convinced myself that once she was accustomed to her new job, then she would have more time for our relationship again. I was being supportive and not overbearing during this time.

I knew our relationship wasn't going to be perfect because that is not possible in today's world. I understood that a great relationship took time to build and it took two people willing to both give it their all for it to be successful. I was committed because I thought she was the one and I loved her.

One night we were at my place around Christmas time and we decided that we were going to get into the Christmas spirit. I was looking forward to our date all week long and could barely contain my excitement. We picked out a couple of Christmas movies, snacks, and drinks and before we could even start the movie or pop the popcorn, she said grudgingly, "Tyler, we need to talk."

I could feel my heart sink into my stomach and I had no idea what she wanted to talk about, but I knew it wasn't good. I took a deep breath and said, "What is on your mind, is everything ok?"

She looked me in my eyes and said, "I am having doubts about this relationship. I just don't have that feeling anymore."

I could feel my heart breaking into a million pieces as the girl I'm in love with doesn't love me back. She noticed that I was crushed by the news and said, "I still want to date you and see if I get those feelings back. I'm just trying to communicate to you how I feel."

As I try and hold back the tears, I work up the courage to say, "Thanks for communicating with me your feelings. I know you've had a lot going on in your life with your new job and this relationship, so I just want us to take things slow. I want you to be happy and for this thing to work."

Jennifer looked at me with relief as she was happy with what I said. "I think the world of you, Tyler. I just don't know why I don't have those feelings I once had. But I agree that we should take things slow and see what happens."

We talked for a few more minutes and seemed to roughly get onto the same page when it came to our relationship. We then watched a Christmas movie and tried to get into the Christmas Spirit.

As the date ended, I walked her to her car and told her to, "Text me when you get home, so I know you're safe."

We hugged and I kissed her. She then got into her car and drove off down the street. As I saw her tail lights drive in the distance, I couldn't help but think how much I love her. But I knew at this moment, I thought that could be the last time I would ever see her. Even though we both said we wanted to continue seeing each other, I knew the end was near. I was crushed and was preparing for the worst.

The following two weeks were the most difficult of my life. I barely got any sleep as I stayed up all night thinking about her and hoping she would come back around. I even would say a prayer or two about it. In a span of a couple of weeks, I went from pure joy at the start of the relationship to chronic depression towards the end. I never went through anything depression related before and was unsure what to do about it. I truly felt like I was being dragged through the mud.

We saw each other once in a while and talked now and again. But I could feel her slipping away. I had a million thoughts cross my mind and the one that kept on coming back was that she said she had feelings for her ex-boyfriend still. I just had to know the outcome of us and couldn't take this pain anymore.

On our next date at her place, we sat down on the couch and began talking. I asked her, "Where are you with us? Anything new?"

"I still feel the same way." She said as she felt attacked for me even bringing it up as she rolled her eyes.

"Look, Jennifer, I want this to work and I think the world of you. But I feel like I'm being dragged through the mud." I said while holding back tears.

She said without emotion, "Well if that is how you feel then we should end this. I don't want you to feel like you're being dragged through the mud."

I was mortified by her mentioning ending our relationship. I then said, "Maybe being dragged through the mud is a bit hyperbolic and that I am overreacting. Let's just continue seeing each other and see what happens."

She nodded her head in agreement. I knew deep down she wanted to end things, but she couldn't bring herself to do it.

Jennifer then needed to get a Christmas gift for a Secret Santa at her job and wanted me to go. Then, afterward, we would get dinner together. If anything, she knew it would be a good distraction from this conversation.

We left her place and went to this home goods store. She started picking up random things to put into a basket for Secret Santa. The whole time I was contemplating whether or not this was worth the pain and suffering I was going through just because I thought she was the one. "Is this depression and lack of sleep worth it?" I thought to myself.

She could tell I was thinking intensely about something and asked, "What are you thinking about?"

To avoid the topic I told her, "Nothing, I'm just hungry." We walked up to the register and she paid for the gifts as I stood there lifelessly. I couldn't do this anymore. I loved this girl, but I didn't love being depressed. "I have to do something!" I thought to myself.

As we walked to her car something came over me. Something I've never felt before. It is unexplainable what I was feeling. I had this inexplicable feeling of self-assurance and felt the need to talk to her. It was supernatural and was like I was being controlled by something. We both got into the car and as soon as we both shut our doors I blurted out, "I can't take this anymore."

She looked over at me and said, "What do you mean?"

I said, "I'm being dragged through the mud and I just can't take it anymore. We need to end things. I can't wait around for you to get these feelings back."

She looked at me and said, "If that is what you want, then let's end things."

She then drove me back to her place where she parked her car and then brought her gifts inside to set on the counter. I gathered my things and then she hugged me. I knew at this moment that she was emotionally gone because she didn't have any emotions and you could sense she was happy to be moving on with her life without me. We said our goodbyes and I went to find my truck.

The walk from her place to my truck was a walk I'll never forget. I felt this peace about me because I knew I didn't have to wait on her any longer. I knew she was gone, but because I knew she was, I had peace. I finally got my answer and didn't have to wait on her anymore.

I got into my truck and I began crying. I was bailing my eyes out because the girl I loved was gone. She was no longer mine and she acted like she didn't even care when it ended. For the first time in my life, I was heartbroken. I sat in my truck for a couple of minutes to gather myself and then I drove home.

The next day I felt better and surprisingly got decent sleep. I thought I would feel worse than I did, but it was because I wasn't being dragged through the mud anymore, I finally had clarity. I figured I would stay at home, think about how to move on, and watch movies in my room all day before I had to go to work the next day.

Then, it hit me, I will have to see Jennifer's dad, Ed, tomorrow at work. I was not prepared to see him at all and wanted to call out sick for the next week. I thought to myself, "How can I see him tomorrow after his daughter just broke my heart?" It was going to be awkward between us and seeing him would remind me of Jennifer.

The next day I got the courage to go to work. I did not want to go to work but it would be a good distraction as long as I stay away from Ed. I walked into my office and nobody was around. "Thank God," I mumbled to myself. I booted up my computer, went over, and poured myself a cup of coffee. As soon as I got back into my office my friend John came in and sat down. He asked me how Jennifer and I were doing. (He was the only one at work who knew that I was dating Ed's daughter because he was with Ed when he gave me her number on the sticky note.) I had the most giant frog in my throat and couldn't speak. As I held back tears, John recognized that something terrible had happened. He said, "oh no, she broke up with you?"

I nodded my head, yes and you could feel the sadness that he felt for me. John cared for me and wanted Jennifer and me to work out. He was close with Ed and told me, "I'll keep Ed away from you for a couple of days."

I told him, "Thank you!" He understood that I needed some time away from Ed. I'm sure Ed did too, but the reassurance from John gave me comfort.

5

My Good Friend, John

Jeremiah 29:11

"For I know the plans I have for you," declares the Lord, "plans to prosper you and not to harm you, plans to give you hope and a future."

John was a good friend of mine. Although he was about thirty years older than me, we got along great. He had his fair share of heartbreaks in his day, but what stuck out to me the most was the faith that he still had after getting heartbroken over and over again.

He grew up a Catholic in Pennsylvania where he met and married his high school sweetheart. They eventually moved to Colorado because of a job opportunity for John. They had two kids together and seemed to live the perfect life. They had a stunning home, nice cars, and lived in a pleasant area. They treasured going to the race track and viewing all the diverse vehicles that they would watch. They were living the American Dream.

To make a long story short, his wife eventually wanted a divorce from him. John did not want to get divorced as he loved her with all of his heart and never wanted to see her go. She eventually turned the kids against him and he never saw them again. She took every-thing from him; his house, cars, money, and his livelihood. John had to start his life over from the beginning essentially. He had nothing and felt he was at rock bottom.

He had to get a second job in the evenings and early nights to pay for child support and to be able to afford to make a living. On top of working at a major airline as an Aircraft Mechanic, he started work-ing at a central distribution center handling packages. He would work sixteen-hour days for years until his debts were paid off.

I asked about how he felt about his ex-wife after she put him through all of that and he replied, "I hate her for it, but if she would come back into my life, I wouldn't say I would or wouldn't take her back. Love makes you do crazy things, Tyler." I was dumbfounded by his response, but then realized I'd go back to Jennifer if she reached out to me. I loved that woman like John loved his ex-wife. Love makes you do crazy things.

What stuck out to me was that John has kept his relationship with Jesus the entire time. Sure, he'll admit that he had some tough times in the beginning, but he always pursued Christ. John lost everything and that he still loved Jesus shows just how great Jesus must be. He would always tell me, "Look up, all the answers are there." And it would always resonate with me. I never really under-stood Christ until later on, but I knew that by looking up to the heavens and the skies I would find all the answers.

He'd always bring up Jesus and talk about how great He is. At this time in my life I knew Jesus was great and that He loved me, but I didn't fully grasp it. I was curious about Jesus, but I never pursued Him until later on. John watered the seeds of Christ, that were planted by my parents years ago when they introduced me to Him through the church, prayer, and holidays. His pain and suffering weren't for nothing, as he helped me grow in my faith.

Because of John and God's Grace, I was becoming interested in who Christ was.

John met a girl during the time I was dating Jennifer, so we bonded even more. He would come into my office and we'd talk about our weekends with our girlfriends. He was in love and I was in love. We would talk about how different life felt when you loved a girl like how music and food would sound and taste better. When doing mundane chores like going to the grocery store would be fun with them.

Then, the unthinkable happened to John and me. Both of our girls broke up and left us heartbroken within a couple of weeks of each other. I leaned on John for advice during this challenging time because he was a great friend and he had the best advice. He has been down this road before and during the whole time he would tell me, "Look up!" He also told me all the time that "I pray for you every day, Tyler." That always resonated with me too. I would tell him the same and I would start praying for him—something I have never done for someone before. I prayed for him to find the love of his life and that he was happy.

When going through the pain you always wanted it just to end and go back to before you met the girl that broke your heart. But I needed growth and I knew it. John always said, "There was a purpose for everything God does in your life. You might not see it now, but you will eventually."

6

Living In Fear

1 Peter 5:7

"Cast all your anxiety on Him because He cares for you."

The following couples of months, after Jennifer left me, were the hardest of my life. I went through severe depression and didn't know how to deal with it. I would wake up pondering to myself, "What is the point of life?" I never thought about committing suicide or harming myself, but I understood why someone would turn to that. It is challenging and you won't know until you go through it. Thankfully I didn't turn to alcohol or hardcore drugs to deal with the pain, but instead I decided to try and get through it on my own. I didn't talk to anybody about my depression because I didn't want people to worry about me or treat me differently.

When your life is in its darkest hour, you don't think with a sober mind. You don't see the beauty that this world has to offer because your brain is wired with a negative attitude. I wasn't sure how to get out of this depression and anxiety I was feeling, but I was going to try. I had the typical attitude of a masculine man that was going to take care of this in private. I didn't want people to worry about me or feel sorry for me. I was too proud for that, even though I could have used support during this time.

Growing up I didn't believe that depression was a real thing. I knew dreadful things happened to people, but my mindset was that it was the cost-of-living life. I figured that you should be happy, no matter what because this life offers you an abundance of virtuous things. I would often hear about how some of my cousins and friends were depressed, but I figured that life was too great to feel like that. I used to think to myself, "Just be happy! Life is what you make it." I was immature, dumb, and naïve. Depression is a real thing and something that I had to go through.

I began my journey by reading literature on relationship advice for men to try and better themselves in the aspect of dating. I lacked experience when it came to dating and I thought that is why Jennifer left me. I read around ten different books that all had similar advice, the female was supposed to play the feminine role and you as the man were supposed to play the masculine role. I genuinely believe that is why God brought a man and a woman into this world. It makes a lot of sense to me and is something I practice right now.

I spent countless hours reading these self-help relationship books and watching videos trying to get a better gauge of how I should act around women. I knew that I needed to improve because where I lacked experience, I also needed more confidence. I was determined to better myself by becoming a better man in a relationship.

When diving into these self-help books I thought to myself, "I'm heartbroken now and don't want it ever to happen again. If Jennifer does come back, I want to be the best version of myself so she would never leave me again." My motives were to win her back because I was in love and didn't want anyone else. I was a hundred percent certain she was the one for me. I just needed to grow as a man.

Reading these books and watching videos online about this topic lasted for about six months. I started to feel better when I would indulge in this matter because I felt like I had a plan. I thought I have grown as a person and was ready for the next chapter of my life. But I was still living in fear that I would never find love. It weighed on my mind and would bring me down a rabbit hole of severe depression and anxiety each time I thought about it. Whether Jennifer would come back or somebody new, I was scared I'd be alone forever.

I used to pray to God, "I pray for Jennifer to come back into my life and that you open her heart to me. I've spent hours upon hours reading these self-help relationship books and feel confident I can win her over now." This was my ploy to God that I am good enough now and that He should bring her back into my life.

I prayed to God often during my time of depression, anxiety, and living in fear. I didn't know who God was, but I sure prayed to Him because I believed in Him. My friend, John, always prayed to God, so I figured I should start doing it too. I never pursued Him because He wasn't as important to me as finding love in my life. I wanted a wife more than anything and I felt like it was never going to happen. I treated God as a wishing well and didn't think that much more of Him. I figured if I am good, then God will give me what I want.

I used to briefly indulge in some astrology, manifesting, and meditation to escape the depression. I would pray to God, but then when nothing would happen, I would meditate by manifesting my future wife to come to me. I am a Virgo and would see if girls were compatible with me with their astrology signs. I would try to manifest people, places, and things into my life because I thought the universe would listen. I had the mindset that I had to do this by myself and manifesting was just that. I tried to speak into existence that I would find love in a spouse one day soon. I was trying to play God in my life. I was very prideful and thought I could make it happen since God isn't answering me.

When the manifesting, astrology, and meditation weren't working after a brief attempt at it, I gave it up and started praying again. I never told anybody about this attempt at those things, but, my friend, John, came up to me in my office one afternoon and kept saying to me, "Keep looking up. All the answers are right there. Keeping praying." It was like he knew I was getting away from God and indulging in those other things and had to say something. I was grateful because after a while of praying consistently over a couple of days, I would feel better. The depression would subside some and I had hope again.

Regardless, praying would help the depression to an extent, but it wouldn't subside completely. I could see that prayer was helping, but my pride wouldn't let me pursue Christ. I was stuck in the world and figured I could figure this out on my own.

I ended up meeting another girl, named Amanda, and we dated for a couple of months. She was a nice gal who shared a lot in common with me, but I knew she wasn't the one right away. We were both looking for different things in our dating life, but I went along with it anyways. I was desperate to find love and started to lower my expectations. I am not saying she wasn't a high-value woman or that she was less than me, but rather that we didn't see eye to eye when it came to dating. We only dated for a couple of months and if anything, she distracted me from the depression I was going through.

When I was dating Amanda, I would often try and bring it up to Ed at work because I thought he would tell, his daughter, Jennifer, and that she would get jealous. The truth is, I never had feelings for Amanda, I just liked the attention that she gave me and was using her to make Jennifer jealous. It was a horrible thing for me to do to her and I regret it. I no longer communicate with her and it wasn't because we had a messy breakup, but instead I think we both moved on and didn't look back.

After dating Amanda, the depression and anxiety came back as they did before. I was living in fear and everywhere I went to try and find the love I wanted I would fail. It was hard to meet the type of woman I was looking for and the only place I kept coming back to was online dating. I went on a couple of dates here and there, but the profiles that people made never matched who they were as a person. It was challenging and the failed dates just added fuel to the fire of the fear I was living in.

7

Second Chance

Proverbs 16:4
*"The LORD works out everything to its proper
end— even the wicked for a day of disaster."*

Jennifer reached out to me about seven months after breaking my heart. It was a text message about her father doing something funny at work that he must have told her about. I know she was trying to find a reason to text me and didn't know what else to say. We ended up texting for a couple of messages back and forth until she stopped replying. I was beyond excited that she texted me after not hearing from her for several months. I couldn't hold my emotions in and had to tell someone about it.

I ran into John at work the next day and we began to converse. He noticed the giant smile on my face and the upbeat vibe that has been missing for the past couple of months. He asked me, "What's going on with you?"

I replied, "Guess who texted me yesterday?"

He looked me in the eyes with a serious face and said, "She did not, did she?"

I replied joyfully, "She sure did John and I am pumped about it!"

John looked at me like I was some psychopath and didn't understand why I was so happy. We began conversing about the text messages we sent back and forth and you could tell by his reaction that he didn't like what he was hearing.

"Tyler, you know she is just fishing to see if you'll bite her line?" John said in a serious tone.

'What do you mean by that?" I replied puzzled.

"She just broke your heart several months ago and didn't care at the time. What makes you think it will be better this time?" said John.

I began to think to myself about how I have all this knowledge now about dating and relationships with those splendid self-help books I've been reading.

"I'm a changed man! Maybe we just met at the wrong time. I bet she misses me" I replied intently.

Jennifer and I had texted each other on and off for a week or so at this point. It felt good to talk to her again, but it wasn't like it was amounting to anything substantial. I think at this time she missed me, but was afraid of what I thought about her. After reading those self-help books, I learned that I needed to play it cool and not be over-emotional, so I did.

A couple more weeks went by and I was sitting in my office staring at my computer monitor. I was looking at booking a flight to Tampa Bay, Florida for my family's yearly vacation. Everyone had their ticket purchased, but I worked for the airline, so I flew for free on Standby. While I was looking at flights, Ed walked into my office and glanced at my computer monitor. He asked me, "where are you going?"

I told him, "Tomorrow I'm going to Tampa Bay with the family! We're going on a long weekend vacation."

He then laughed out loud. "What is so funny?" I said to him.

"Jennifer and I are going there tomorrow as well after work. When do you fly back?" said Ed.

I thought he was joking because there was no way he was traveling to the same city I was in and during the same time I was. "I get back Sunday evening," I said.

He then walked out of my office and I didn't see him the rest of the day. I was sure he was joking around with me.

Later that night as I'm packing for my trip, I get a text message from Jennifer. It read, "I'll see you in Tampa."

I replied and asked her, "Are you being serious?"

She replied, "I am! I probably won't see you there, but I think were on the same flight coming home."

At this exact moment, I feel a sense of joy that I haven't felt in months and I immediately look up and think, "Thank you, God." I thought this was my chance to get her back. I know she is interested in me again, but she is just afraid to put it all out there again.

While in Tampa Bay, Florida, Jennifer was blowing up my phone. We messaged each other back and forth the whole trip and I was enjoying every minute of it. You could tell she was interested; it reminded me of when we first started dating. I was ecstatic and couldn't wait to catch the flight home knowing she'd be there. I couldn't wait to see her again.

The day had arrived and my family was on our way to the airport. We dropped off the rental car, checked our bags, and headed for airport security. As we stood in line, I had this feeling that God was bringing us back together because He wanted us to be together. I was sure of it! I take off my shoes and put my carry-on bag onto the conveyor belt. I walk through the metal detector, look up, and see her in the distance. We make eye contact immediately and she smiles at me. I think to myself, "Oh, how I've missed that beautiful smile of hers." We then talk for a few minutes before my family departs for the gate. I tell her, "I'll see you at the gate!" as she stood there waiting for her dad to finish going through airport security.

We get to the gate on a relatively open flight and sit down near the window. I catch up with Ed and Jennifer at the front gate while they were checking in. Come to find out my seat is a middle seat between them. Ed must have pulled a fast one and asked the front desk agent to change my seat to get us to sit next to each other. I know he liked me and wanted me to date his daughter again, so he went out of his way to get us to be close during the four-hour flight. Let's say I didn't mind sitting in the middle seat this time.

As we get to our seats and waited for the plane to taxi away, Ed tells us that he is going to try and sleep during the flight and jokingly says, "Don't wake me up!"

Jennifer and I laugh and agreed to keep it down for him. As the plane takes off Jennifer starts talking to me immediately. She wanted to catch up. We chatted, laughed, and had a good conversation for what seemed like thirty minutes as the plane touched down in Denver. It was the fastest four-hour flight of my entire life.

We exited the plane and headed for the train to take us to baggage claim. At this time Jennifer and I got separated because of the big crowds. I looked around baggage claim for her to no avail. As I headed to my truck in the parking lot speculating where she ended up going, I get a text message from Jennifer stating, "It was good to see you, Tyler! I had fun sitting next to you on our flight home!" I then replied by asking her out on a date and she was more than excited to go. I thought this was it, as I said to myself "I've got this girl back into my life again!" The depression melted away instantly.

A week later I drive to her house to pick her up and we head over to a local brewery. The date ended up going well and what got me excited is that you can sense that she was into me. It almost felt like she was into me more than I was into her. "I rate this date five out of five stars! Wait, actually four out of five stars. I don't want you to think you are perfect or anything!" She said flirtatiously. As I drove her home you could tell that she had a great time because she was already planning the next time we would see each other.

The following week I decided to do something unique for our date. I was going to surprise her. I loaded up my truck with blankets, pillows, and a cooler full of sandwiches, snacks, and a couple of her favorite beers. I picked her up at her house and we started driving down the street. She asked me, "Where are you taking me?"

I told her, "You'll see soon enough!"

We pulled into an empty parking lot where you can see the mountains in the distance with the sun about to set. I parked and brought the cooler, blankets, and pillows into the bed of my truck. I began to climb into the back and she said, "What are we doing?"

I said, "We are having a picnic in the back of my truck while the sun sets."

You could tell right away that she wasn't totally into the idea, but she climbed in anyway. We sat there and ate our sandwiches; all I noticed was how quiet she was.

"Is everything ok? You seem distant."

She looked at me and said, "I don't know, I'm not sure whom I should date."

I was puzzled about what she just said. "Why do you say that?" I told her.

"This was a great idea, I'm just kind of embarrassed about it. I know you like to do these kinds of things, but it is not for me." She said sadly.

"Let's go grab a drink somewhere close by then!" I suggested as my desperate attempt to win her over.

She agreed and we left the parking lot. I couldn't help but think to myself that something deeper was going on with her. It seems she was suggesting that she didn't want to date me. Why would she say "I'm not sure whom I should date"? I brushed the idea off and focused on enjoying the rest of the date.

After we finished our date that night, I dropped her off at her house and drove home. Compared to the previous date, Jennifer was not engaged at all. I could tell she was having her doubts already. I went back into the depression mode that I had before because I knew this was the beginning of the end.

We ended up going on just one more date a few weeks later and she ended up ending things with me. I began to try and move on over the next couple of months, but it wasn't easy. Depression was always there and was something I just got used to over time. At this point in my life, I had no idea where to turn, but none other than the self-help relationship books that I read before. I studied these books harder than I ever did before.

I remember having conversations with John about what happened with Jennifer and me, and all he could say was, "Keep looking up!" Of course, he told me, "You should never talk to her again because she is just going to break you again." I wholeheartedly agreed. It seemed like he was mad at her for what she did to me. She did play with my heart on two separate occasions, but in reality, I let her.

8

Goodbye

Ecclesiastes 3:1

"There is a time for everything, and a season for every activity under the heavens"

A couple more months passed and I was starting to feel better. I still had depression here and there, but it wasn't as bad as it was before. I ended up transferring departments within the company to a new location on the other side of town. I was indifferent about transferring, but it felt like a fresh start. Something I had trouble coping with was that I wouldn't see John every day. He gave me sound advice and was a good friend of mine. He was sad to see me go but said, "God has a plan for you. Your season here is coming to an end because He wants you over there now."

During my second week at my new job, I get a notification on my phone. It was a text message from Jennifer stating, "how are you doing?"

I remember looking at my phone and becoming angry at her. I asked myself, "Why can't she leave me alone, I was feeling better. I was just moving on." I knew she was fishing for attention from me.

Nothing good will come from her if I pursue her again. I put the phone back into my pocket and carried on with my day.

After a couple of hours, I replied with a message along the lines of "Leave me alone", but in a friendlier tone. She then apologized for messaging me and for playing with my heart in the past. She wanted to be friends with me, but I wasn't having it. She just wanted the attention that I used to give her in the past. I was so mad; I didn't even reply to her apology. I ended up blocking her number and all of her social media accounts. I felt a peace that I haven't felt in years when I did that, something I should have done months ago. It needed to be done for my mental health. I almost thought I leveled up like I was in a video game.

My new boss, Steve, started working in our department a couple of weeks after I started. He was in his mid-fifties, married, and had children. His children had children making him a grandfather. He was a gentle giant that loved softball, Texas, his family, and Jesus. We talked here and there, but mostly it was about sports. I always wanted to ask him about Jesus and why he loved Him but figured I better not talk about religion at work, especially to someone I didn't know that well. I didn't know at this moment in time, but Steve would later have an enormous impact on my life.

A couple of weeks into my new job, I decided I was going to try and get back out into the dating pool again. I downloaded a couple of different dating applications on my phone and made a couple of profiles. I never had success with dating applications but I decided to try again, this time I have some experience. I went on a couple of different dates, but nothing amounted to anything. Every time I had a bad date, I would start thinking about Jennifer immediately. It made me miss her terribly. I almost messaged her on a couple of different instances, but never pulled the trigger. I tried to stay positive and figured the right girl will come along soon enough.

One day at work, I was cleaning and organizing an area by myself when the song, "Done" by Chris Janson came on the radio. I sat down on a chair close by and began listening to the lyrics.

"The first time I saw you, done
Like the first dance was through, I was done
That one kiss, I knew
There was nothing I wouldn't do
Just to give you
That house on a hill with a four-plank around it
Every last breath 'til the last star is counted
Just say the word girl, paint me, you're perfect
I won't quit 'til the good Lord says my work is done
Like a faded-out song on the radio, done
Like the cowboy gets the girl when the credits roll
I'll give you a lifetime of days in the sun
Whatever you need and you want
I won't stop 'til it's done"

I began to cry immediately after listening to this part of the song. The singer, Chris Janson, was in love with a girl and wanted her to have a picture-perfect life. He was going to do everything in his power to make it happen. This is what I wanted all along to do for a girl I loved. I wanted to lay down my life just so the girl I married would be happy and have everything she could ever want. I wasn't going to stop until the good Lord said my work was done.

Shockingly, I wasn't even thinking about Jennifer during this song, but rather a girl I haven't met yet. I realized Jennifer wasn't the one I was meant to be with, so I knew this was a step in the right direction because I was getting over her.

Getting over Jennifer was no easy task, but over the next couple of months, it got easier. I thought about her a lot less and wouldn't get depressed when I did think about her. The depression and anxiety were still there, but not as severe as it was before because I was distracted by my job and the time was passing by. It helped that I didn't see Jennifer's Dad, Ed, anymore because he would just remind me of her. Cutting her out of my life was another reason why I was starting to get over her because I had no other choice. She wasn't the one and it made me move on.

During this time, I could feel myself leveling up like I was in a video game. I felt better about my situation because I knew I would learn from it and that the right girl would eventually come around to me. I still wanted to find love more than anything and would stop at nothing to find it. I just felt my options were stretched thin and I didn't know where to go. But it wasn't going to stop my pursuit of trying to find the love of my life.

9

My Second Love

On a fall Sunday early afternoon, I decided to message this girl on social media that I've had my eyes on for the last couple of years. We had a lot of mutual friends, but we never met each other before in person. She didn't post a lot, which I liked, and when she did, they were conservative photos. She smiled in every picture and wouldn't dress in a floozy way. She never even posted a picture of her in her swimsuit. I liked that about her and thought she might be a good match for me. She was beautiful and seemed to have her life figured out, but I knew nothing about her other than she was a nurse. She was the type of girl that your mom would approve of. Her name was Haley.

A couple of hours later, Haley replied to my message apologizing for the delay in her response. We messaged back and forth for the next couple of days until I found the right opportunity to ask her out on a date. She seemed delighted about the idea of going on a date and said yes. The upcoming weekend we agreed to meet at a brewery close to her place.

The upcoming weekend as I got into my truck, I thought to myself, "I haven't been this excited to go on a date since Jennifer." I arrive at the brewery and park my truck nearby. I get out and head in the direction of the front door. I was the first to arrive, so I stood near the door and waited for her. After a few minutes, I look up and see her walking towards me. My first thought about her was that she was gorgeous and I immediately get butterflies in my stomach. She gave off an innocent vibe that I found undeniably attractive. She looked even better in person than in the pictures that she posted on social media; I was blown away. We introduced ourselves and hugged each other. I opened the brewery door for her, she smiled and we walked inside. We found the bar and headed in that direction. Once we ordered our beers, we found a spot near the firepit outside. We sat down and started asking questions about each other. I could tell that she was nervous at the start but would get more comfortable as the conversation went on. I could tell early that we had a lot in common.

As the night went along, she said, "I want to buy you something to eat at the food truck out front! What sounds good to you?"

I told her, "That is nice of you, but let me buy since I was the one to ask you out on a date!"

She said, "Let me buy since you have bought the drinks. It is only fair."

I finally gave in to her demands after a couple more failed attempts of trying to get myself to buy. She went and got us some chicken tenders and fries with ranch dressing. I was impressed with her how she wanted to buy food after I bought the drinks. Haley was a special kind of girl and she was someone I could see myself going on another date with. I've been on many dates where the girl doesn't even bother to offer to buy or split the bill. I always pay, but the offer is always a nice gesture.

As the date ended, I paid my tab and walked her to her car. I hugged her and told her to, 'Text me when you get home, so I know you're safe."

She agreed and got into her car. As I walked to my truck, I looked up to the sky and asked God, "Is she the one I'm supposed to be with?"

For the first time I have been on a date since Jennifer broke my heart, I thought I found someone that had great potential. I was ecstatic and couldn't wait to see her again. I liked my date with Haley and I had a great time. I thought she was beautiful and we seemed to have a lot in common.

As the weeks went by, Haley and I started seeing each other often. We messaged each other all day long and shared calls at night before we both went to bed. The conversations didn't feel forced and again, we had a lot in common—our political affiliation, lifestyle, music taste, Christianity and so much more. The more I saw her, it seemed the more she was falling for me. I was falling in love with her. I couldn't wait to see what the future brought for the both of us.

A couple of months later on Valentine's Day, I arrive at her house to pick her up to go to dinner with a dozen red roses in my hands. As I hand them to her, you could see the smile on her face light up the driveway. She didn't date much in her life and didn't get many flowers, so I think she enjoyed getting them from me. She deserved those flowers as she was the sweetest girl I have ever met.

We walk over to my truck and I open her door for her. She smiled and said, "thank you, Ty."

As she got into the passenger seat. I shut the door and walk around to the driver's side. She had a smile on her face that I haven't seen from her before. She was overjoyed to get flowers and to get them from me.

We arrive at the restaurant and walk up to the front door. I open the door for her and we walk inside. There was a fifteen-minute wait, so we decided to sit down in the waiting area. She starts talking about her day and how the host of the show, "The Bachelor" fell victim to cancel culture for defending someone that used to be on the show. I think he did it to show support to them and tried to make people realize that people make mistakes. Haley was sad about it because she loves the show. She always wanted to watch the show with me, but I never could because of a work-schedule conflict.

The hostess calls out the name, "Tyler." Haley and I proceed to the front where the hostess guides us to our table. We had good conversations while we ate our meals. It was an enjoyable date with a beautiful girl. I was falling deeply in love with her and couldn't wait to see where this was headed.

We left the restaurant and went to our next stop, her favorite brewery. We went inside and ordered our drinks from the bartender. We were the only ones there, which seemed strange because it was a Saturday. We drank about half of our drinks and Haley says shivering, "Why is it so cold in here? It is like the heater doesn't work."

It turns out she was right. The bartender apologized for the heater not working. I remote start my truck to warm it up and then pay the tab at the bar. We exit the brewery and head for my truck. We sit in the warm truck for a couple of minutes to warm up and she says, "Want to go back to my place to watch movies? You can meet my parents."

"That sounds like fun," I said.

I was overjoyed because I knew that meeting someone's parents was a monumental step in the relationship. She must have liked me if she wanted me to meet them.

We arrive at her place and walk into the front door where I am greeted by two Bernese Mountain dogs. I pet them, take off my shoes, and set them by the front door. I walk through the hallway and see Haley's parents and younger sister sitting on the couch in the living room. Haley introduces us to each other and I could tell right away that they were wholesome people. I can see why Haley was such a great girl because she was raised in a great home by some great people. We chatted for roughly half an hour before they ended up going to bed.

Haley then picked a movie out, turned the fireplace on, and found the most oversized blanket that they had. We cuddled up on the couch and watched a romantic movie. About halfway through the movie, Haley fell asleep while laying on my chest and I remember thinking how happy I was at that point. I shed a tear of happiness because I felt I was with the one I would be with forever. I looked up to the sky and said," Thank you, God!"

As the date ended, Haley walked me to the front door and thanked me for the date tonight. She kissed me goodbye and told me, "Text me when you get home, so I know you're safe."

I loved when she said that to me because I knew she cared about me. I didn't want to leave her because I was enjoying her company. I had to wait until the following weekend to see her because our work schedules conflicted with each other. I was barely out the front door and I already missed her.

On the drive home I cried tears of joy because I think I found someone that I loved and they reciprocated it back to me. I said, "Thank you God" probably twenty different times. At this point, I was entirely in love with Haley and was excited to see where it was going to go. "I know there is a reason for you God, to bring Haley into my life!" All the pain and suffering I went through the last couple of years seemed to be paying off. I was in love with Haley.

TYLER MATTHEW GEBHARDT

10

Heartbroken, Again

> **2 Corinthians 12:9**
>
> *"But he said to me, "My grace is sufficient for you, for my power is made perfect in weakness." Therefore, I will boast all the more gladly about my weaknesses, so that Christ's power may rest on me."*

Throughout the work week, I was contemplating whether I should ask Haley to be my girlfriend or not. I figured she thought we were already a couple and this was just a formality to give us the title of being in a relationship together. But, on the other hand, we were taking things slow and I didn't want to scare her off. I was in a dilemma and didn't know what to do. The self-help books told me to wait for her to bring it up, but I loved this girl and wanted her to be mine. I would ask several people that I thought would give me good advice throughout the week and steer me in the right direction.

My mom told me, "If you go any slower, you'll start to go backward."

My friend John said, "tell her how you feel. If she gets scared off, then it wasn't part of God's plan for your life."

My close coworker, Violeta said "Ask her to be your girlfriend, why would she say no to you? You just met her parents!"

Everyone had the same idea, so I decided to run with it and began planning our next date. I was a hundred percent certain this was the right move because I knew she was into me. It seems like a match made in Heaven.

One week after Valentine's Day, Haley and I got together to make breakfast for dinner as a date. She arrived at my place early, so we decided to go to a brewery nearby to grab a drink before it was time to eat. As we head to the restaurant, I thought to myself, "This was my chance to ask her to be my girlfriend." She was beautiful, sweet, big-hearted, and had a great job. We had a lot in common and great chemistry. Dating her almost felt like it was too good to be true.

We arrive at the brewery parking lot and I became nervous because I was about to ask her to be my girlfriend. I get out and walk around my truck to her. She grabs my hand and we proceed to the door. As we get inside, we walk up to the bar and order our drinks. We find a table nearby and start conversing. I wait for the perfect moment to ask her.

I said, "Haley, I like you a lot and think we have a lot in common. The chemistry is off the charts and I think we'd make an awesome couple. The kind of couple that people would look at us and...."

She interrupts me, "Tyler, I know what you're about to ask me and I don't know if I'm ready for that yet"

I nod my head in agreement. She says, "If I was younger, I would say yes, but I've got to be certain before I jump in."

Then, I say, "Let's forget I even brought it up!"

She agrees, but I couldn't wrap my head around it. I thought she was all in as well, but apparently, she wasn't ready yet. Maybe she just needed more time before she jumped into this. I know she was hurt in the past by her ex-boyfriend and perhaps that is why she was scared to jump in.

As we head back to my place, I could sense she was in a mentally different place. Her whole mood changed and wasn't engaged in our date as much.

We arrived back at my place and started making breakfast for dinner. She was in charge of the chocolate chip pancakes and cutting up the fruit, whereas, I was in charge of the eggs, bacon, and pouring orange juice into glasses. While cooking, I would try to flirt with her or start a conversation and she would play along, but it seemed she only did it to be friendly and not make it awkward.

After we ate our breakfast for dinner, we cleaned up the dishes and then headed for the couch to watch a movie. I sat down on the right side of the couch, where we always sat together so that we could cuddle and Haley sat on the left side, by herself, distant from me.

I thought to myself, "All I did was ask her to be my girlfriend and now she is shutting me out?"

As the movie started playing, I got us a blanket and asked, "Do you want to cuddle with me?"

She nodded her head yes and slid over close to me on the couch. She got under the blanket with me and I kissed her forehead.

About ten minutes later she got out of from under the blanket and slid down the couch again. I asked her, "Is everything ok? You seem like something is on your mind."

She assured me, "Everything is fine." About another ten minutes passed and I decided to pause the movie.

I said, "Haley, what is going on?"

She paused for a couple of seconds to gather her thoughts, "I just don't know... Dating you was going so well and then all of the sudden... I just don't know."

"Are you having doubts?" I said anxiously.

She couldn't look me in the eyes, but nodded her head yes, a couple of times and stopped.

"You're a great guy Tyler and I don't know why I feel like this." She said to me.

When Jennifer broke up with me, I always thought about what I could have said or how I could have acted differently. I would go over scenarios in my head and then would come up with the perfect things to say. I didn't think I'd ever need to carry out this exact scenario again. But here we are.

"Haley, I've got three things I want to say to you. Number one, thank you for communicating your feelings to me. I know that isn't easy to do. I know I kind of had to pry an answer out of you, but you still told me the truth. So, thank you. Number two, I need a girl that I don't have to worry about ever wanting to leave me. There are going to be ups and downs during a relationship with someone and I need someone that is going to be with me, no matter what. I need someone that is going to be scared to lose me. Which brings me to my final point..." I said poised.

As I take a deep inhale and look Haley in the eyes, I say, "Number three, if you're having doubts this early into our relationship, or whatever we are, I think it's time to end things between us."

She looked up at me with a blank stare on her face and nodded her head yes.

"I can't go through another relationship where I have to question every single day, whether the girl I'm dating is into me or not. It is not worth my sanity to go through that." I said holding back tears.

She said, "I'm sorry, Tyler. I just don't know why I don't have feelings for you anymore."

I said to her, "You can't control whom you fall for. It is what it is. We are better off ending this now before we waste years of our lives together trying to fake our way through it."

Haley then smiled and said, "Thank you for understanding."

As she gathered her things, I try and hold back tears and think to myself, "Here we go again..." I open the front door and we proceed to her car. We give each other one last hug and she says, "Thanks Tyler. You really are a great guy."

I said, "Haley, I hope you find someone one day and that they treat you well. You deserve it. Text me when you get home, so I know you got there safe"

She then got into her car and drove off down the street. I could see her taillights disappearing in the distance as I begin to break down crying. I went inside and sat on the couch where it all just happened. I sat there motionless and tried to process what just happened.

Twenty minutes later I get a text from her saying, "Thank you for being you!" with a heart emoji. After reading the text from her, I completely lose it again and cry. I couldn't believe what had just happened. She seemed like she was invested in me and overnight she changed her mind.

I kept thinking back to those self-help relationship books I used to comb through religiously and thought I had all the answers. I thought I followed them for the most part, although I would mess up once in a while and veer away from the points the book made, it just showed I had to be one hundred percent perfect to keep a girl around me. How was everyone else doing it? I was utterly at a loss and went into a chronic depression again. But it wouldn't last for long.

11

My Good Friend, Steve

> *2 Corinthians 5:20*
> *"We are therefore Christ's ambassadors, as though God were making his appeal through us. We implore you on Christ's behalf: Be reconciled to God."*

I worked with Steve and would talk to him every day. He was the supervisor of my department. Coworkers would often tease me for being in the boss's office all the time for brown-nosing with him, but in reality, I was in his office building a friendship with him. Steve was a good man and a devoted follower of Christ. Steve had a unique upbringing. He was born and raised in Kentucky. His mother passed away when he was five years old and was raised by his father. His father would often brag about how he would never say a curse word, but would then proceed to beat his son. His father would have a different woman every single week running around the house, neglecting his kids, and would have racist tendencies. Although his dad meant well, he did not give Steve the best living conditions growing up.

Later on, Steve married his wife when he was twenty-two years old in Kentucky. A couple of years later he moved to Texas and had two kids, a girl, and a boy. He served our nation in the Air Force for a couple of years after tours in Afghanistan. He started a Prison Ministry called Colorado Sports Reach where he would travel the country and play softball in prisons with the inmates. They would play a game and afterward, they would all gather around to talk about Jesus.

I would often go to my boss, Steve, and talk to him about my depression and anxiety. He would often talk about his Prison Ministry and Jesus. I was curious about who Jesus was. I knew Jesus was a great man, but I didn't fully grasp who He was. I didn't understand what He has done for me in my life or what being a faithful Christian is.

Steve would help me through this tough time just like my friend, John, did before him. Steve knew Jesus and wanted me to know Him too. I knew Jesus was a great man, but I didn't fully grasp who He was. I didn't understand what He has done for me in my life or what being a faithful Christian is.

12

Born Again

John 3:3

"Jesus replied, "Very truly I tell you, no one can see the kingdom of God unless they are born again."

A couple of weeks after Haley broke my heart, I was feeling hopeless and would question if this life was even worth living. I would never think about committing suicide or harming myself, but the pain I was feeling was immense. I was just in a rough spot in my life and wanted it to be over with. The depression and anxiety were eating me alive. I couldn't sleep at night and didn't want to get out of bed in the morning. I was at rock bottom with nowhere to go.

The depression was back in full force like it was a couple of years ago after Jennifer broke my heart. I had no idea how to shake it or what to do to help me get through it. I was completely lost and unsure where to go. Depression is something to take very seriously because it affects everything you do in your life. I had lost my motivation to function and didn't want to get out of bed every morning. I didn't talk to the people that I loved in my life about my depression because I didn't want them to worry about me. I needed help and didn't know where to go.

One day after work, I was at home laying on the couch staring at the ceiling thinking about how much I hated my life. I went through two heartbreaks in about thirty months. I wanted to love and be loved, but that seemed to be out of the question. I have been burned too many times and figured being loved by someone else wasn't in the cards for me. I asked God, "If you really loved me, you wouldn't have taken Haley from me." As I teared up, I said, "I can't take this anymore. I am begging you to help me! Show me where I need to go!" I was being honest with God about how I felt. I was mad at Him for taking her away from me. I didn't understand why I was being punished.

The next day I was scrolling through Instagram and a 'Suggested Profile' popped up on my feed. It was John Kennedy Vaughn, an author, of the book, "The Right Fight: How to Live a Loving Life." Many his posts talked about his book and how he has found the right way to live a life full of love. I did not read much at all because it honestly was boring to me, but decided to make an impulse purchase and bought the book. I didn't know it was a Christian book until after I purchased it, but that didn't matter to me. I was desperate to leave this pain behind and move on with my life. This book seemed like it could help me.

I went to a quiet place at my home and started reading "The Right Fight." One of the first chapters in the book was a story about how John Kennedy Vaughn was a competitive water jump skier. In practice, he trained for his competitions and kept failing. He would mess up and it left him living in fear. He feared that he wasn't good enough to be in this competition and would let himself down. The story takes a quick turn when he is just about to start his match when a moment of clarity came over him. He thought it didn't matter what the results were, but rather if he did this for Christ, then he would enjoy it. He started living in love instead of fear and end up winning the competition.

It was at this moment that I started to see who Jesus really was. I began to make sense of Him. "The Right Fight: How to Live a Loving Life." By John Kennedy Vaughn changed my perspective on life. He talked about the Fruit of the Spirit and how it was a biblical way to live life the right way.

The next day while on a break at work, I went off to find a quiet place where I could finish the book. I found a spot in a room on the third floor that had a window that could see out into the distance for a couple of miles. I sat down and eagerly started reading since I only had a couple of chapters left.

As I finished reading "The Right Fight," I began to cry. I cried like I had been saving up my tears for decades. It was like my entire life was a lie and that Christ had all the answers.

Galatians 5:22-23

"But the fruit of the Spirit is love, joy, peace, patience, kindness, goodness, faithfulness, gentleness, self-control; against such things there is no law."

To live a loving life, you needed to have things traits from Galatians 5:22-23 and they needed to be rooted in Christ. Those who are in Jesus Christ stand out from unbelievers in that they have been gifted with the Holy Spirit, empowering them to bear fruit. I was living my life the exact opposite way with anger, rudeness, envy, pride, unforgiveness, boastfulness, and selfishness. God pointed out to me that I needed to change my practices because I was living the wrong way. If that isn't love, I don't know what is.

The day before I prayed to God, *"I can't take this anymore. I am begging you to help me! Show me where I need to go!"* he answered with "The Right Fight: How to Live a Loving Life." By John Kennedy Vaughn. The depression and anxiety were taken away from me and were replaced with joy, peace, and hope. It was a miracle and something I'll remember for the rest of my life. It was one of the first times that I noticed God answering one of my prayers. He was with me in my lowest place and when I reached out for help, he delivered.

God loves me more than I ever even knew. He knew I needed to go to rock bottom for me to become desperate enough to want to change. Before I was heartbroken, I was comfortable and would have never pursued Christ. God knew this, so He broke my heart so that I would want to change. God loves me so He decided to change my life by correcting how I was living my life. He broke me down, so He could build me back up the right way. He was correcting my behavior like my mother or father would have corrected my behavior growing up. If I were doing something wrong my parents would have corrected me because they loved me and wanted the best for me. God did the same thing for me because He loves me. He also took my pain, depression, and anxiety away from me. It was a miracle!

I didn't further pursue Christ at this moment because I was at such a high and I saw the light. I didn't think I needed to do anything else because I saw Jesus for the first time. I thought I had all the answers because this book laid it out for me. I was living with joy, peace, and hope while my depression and anxieties were non-existent.

The high only lasted for about two weeks until hints of depression and anxiety started to appear again. I was desperate and didn't know what to do other than pray because it worked for me before. "God, I hate this depression and I'm praying for you to guide me to where I need to go." I was sick and tired of the depression and anxiety weighing me down. I thought I kicked it for good after reading "The Right Fight: How to Live a Loving Life." By John Kennedy Vaughn, but it was only a Band-Aid. I had thoughts about reading the Bible but figured it was too confusing to read, so I dismissed that quickly.

The next day, I was sitting in the breakroom at work eating my lunch before my shift started when Steve, my boss, walked in. He went to the refrigerator and grabbed a drink. Then, I started walking towards the door.

"Tyler, Christian books are good and all, but you need to read the Bible," Steve said as he walked out of the breakroom. This was bizarre because he usually asked, "How are you doing?" or "How was your weekend?" He didn't even say "Hello" to me. I finished cleaning up my lunch and headed for his office to find him.

I said, "I don't even know where to start. The Bible is confusing and there are hundreds of different versions."

"I suggest you start with the book of John and read the New International Version," Steve said to me.

I had a Bible application on my phone that sent me daily Bible Verses and looked for the book, John, on it.

"I see there is John, 1 John, 2 John, and 3 John. Which one do I read?" I asked him. He chuckled at me because I had zero knowledge of the Bible and he knew it.

Steve said with a smile, "Read John and the other Gospels; Matthew, Mark, and Luke. You'll learn who Jesus is and understand what He did when he was here."

I nodded my head, said "Thank you" and left his office.

I immediately tried to find a quiet area at work where I wouldn't be bothered by anyone. I stumbled upon our garage where we stored all of our vehicles and sat down on an office chair that was there. As I opened up the Bible application on my phone, I could feel this presence and anxiety that I didn't understand. It almost felt like a panic attack. It was like someone or something was trying to keep me from reading the Bible "Why do I feel like this?" I said to myself. I then started reading "John" and got through about halfway through it.

Later on, while talking to Steve about what I was feeling, he said "it is Spiritual Warfare and the devil was attempting to keep you from getting to know Jesus."

That didn't make much sense to me because I didn't understand the devil and his tactics at the time. But I trusted what Steve said and continued my reading of "John." The devil wanted to keep me in the world instead of learning and understanding who Jesus is.

I finished reading John later that evening and I could feel an unexplainable peace around me and I had an idea of why. I haven't felt this way since I finished reading "The Right Fight". I was starting to see the correlation between getting into God's word and the peace I was experiencing. It was all making sense to me and I figured that a life with Christ in it brought peace to me.

God answered my prayer once again. I was desperate for Him to guide me to where I needed to go and by his Grace, He brought the Bible into my life. This time, I didn't stop there but continued pursuing Christ every single day. Christ is my life equaled peace in my mind. I was born again in the Spirit and was on my way to changing my life.

To glorify Him in everything you do. Prayer will change your life. Christ was the love I had been searching for and He was right there the entire time. He took the depression away from me and gave me joy and peace of mind. It is supernatural and hard to explain exactly how it happened, but I found the correlation between Christ in my life and the peace that came with Him.

Mark 11:24

"Therefore, I tell you, whatever you ask for in prayer, believe that you have received it, and it will be yours."

13

People, Places & Things

Isaiah 41:10

"So do not fear, for I am with you; do not be dismayed, for I am your God. I will strengthen you and help you; I will uphold you with my righteous right hand."

God will put people, places, and things in your life when you need them the most. He brings these into my life for many different reasons and sometimes you don't realize what He is doing until after you reflect on it. When I did, I realized that God does love me and has saved me from people, places, and things that I thought I wanted in life. I thought I would have been happy if I had it my way, but it would have been not very good. He always has a better plan for you. He has plans to prosper you and not to harm you, plans to give you hope and a future.

I believe that God brought Jennifer and Haley into my life for a specific reason and that was to break my heart, which then led me into depression. Only then would I become desperate enough to want to change my life. It might sound harsh, but I needed to change my life to live the right way and God knew that. He did it out of love. He knew I needed to go to rock bottom to where I would become desperate, so then I wouldn't have a choice, but to pursue Christ. I was humbled by the Lord, which led me to see the Light that is Jesus Christ.

Through all of this, I matured as a man. I was still a little boy, immature in relationships, naïve in my faith, and lacked a direction in my life. I needed to be refined into a man because I was still lost. To be a man I needed to be humbled and find Christ. God broke me down, to build me back up with Christ as my foundation. If that isn't love, then I don't know what is.

> Isaiah 48:10
>
> "See, I have refined you, though not as silver; I have tested you in the furnace of affliction."

He brought John and Steve into my life to help me through tough times and to push me toward Christ. They were mature Christians that went through their fair share of faith-testing times and gave me solid biblical advice because of it. He knew I needed to be pushed in the right direction and made sure they both would be there for me. God loves me. I don't think it is a coincidence that John and Steve were put into my life either. It could have been other people that would have steered me down the road of destruction.

He brought to me this place in my neighborhood where I would often go and get away from the world. It was a water tower on a hill that overlooks the city of Denver. It was my solitude and a place to recharge my batteries. Whenever I felt down about life, I would go up there, sit and pray to God. I'd stay for as long as my body could take sitting on a small boulder and then push myself to stay a little longer because I never wanted to leave. I never realized it at the time, but I felt closer to God at the water tower and that is why I loved that place.

God knows what is going to happen before it's going to happen. He is God all-knowing and does everything with a purpose that exceeds our knowledge as humans. I've learned that it is best to trust Him completely, which is easier said than done but will save you years of living in uncertainty. Cast all your anxieties onto Him because He cares for you. It takes time and I still struggle with trusting Him completely, but when you do it is worth it, trust me.

One of the most extraordinary things He brought into my life is the YouTube Channel, "Apply God's Word" by Mark Ballenger. He posts videos to help Christians get a better understanding of what God is doing in their life and why He does it. For example, Mark's most popular video is called, "4 Signs God Is Protecting You from a Bad Relationship." He then explains in detail using biblical truth and logic as to why God is doing this. He has thousands of videos ranging from different life topics, but primarily relationship based. He has over six hundred thousand subscribers and posts a couple of times a week. It was the perfect thing I needed during my pursuit of Christ, for it gave me a better understanding and an assurance of what God might be doing in my life.

I have enjoyed listening to Country music over the past decade, so God brought Christian-Country music into my life. A lot of Country artists have songs about God and albums about the Gospel, but a new Christian artist by the name of Anne Wilson stuck out to me. She sings a song called, "My Jesus" and, not by coincidence, it came out about the time I started pursuing Christ when I needed it the most.

"Are you past the point of weary?
Is your burden weighin' heavy?
Is it all too much to carry?
Let me tell you 'bout my Jesus
Do you feel that empty feeling?
'Cause shame's done all its stealin'
And you're desperate for some healin'
Let me tell you 'bout my Jesus
He makes a way where there ain't no way
Rises up from an empty grave
Ain't no sinner that He can't save
Let me tell you 'bout my Jesus
His love is strong and His grace is free
And the good news is I know that He
Can do for you what He's done for me
Let me tell you 'bout my Jesus
And let my Jesus change your life"

The lyrics resonated with me because I was depressed and could relate to this song. I was past the point of weary and the burdens of this life were weighing heavy on me. The song showed me that I needed Jesus and brought everything together for me. I needed help and that help was Jesus.

Josh Turner has always been one of my favorite Country artists and even has a Gospel album, "I Serve a Savior". I got the pleasure of seeing him perform live at the Grizzly Rose in Denver, Colorado a couple of years before I knew Jesus. He played all of his big hit songs like, "Your Man" and "Would You Go with Me", but he also played a couple of songs from his Gospel album that I didn't care for at the time. I hate to admit it, but I couldn't wait for him to finish his Gospel songs and get back to his radio hits. Now, after getting to know Jesus, some of my favorite songs are off of his Gospel album, 'I Saw the Light" and "Long Black Train."

My buddy, Derek, whom I play hockey with, and his wife, Alli, both loved Jesus. I didn't know this until after I came to love Jesus as well. We started doing "Bible Study Plans" together on the Bible application on our phones. It takes about fifteen to twenty minutes every day and there are numerous topics. It is a great way to understand better what you are reading in your Bible and to hear each other's responses. We love doing them together because it also brings up great discussions about the Bible.

"The Chosen" directed by Dallas Jenkins, is a faith-based show about the Gospel of Jesus Christ. It is one hundred percent crowd funded and free for anyone to watch. It is well crafted and the acting is better than you would expect.

One of the most, if not the most, essential things brought into my life is Prayer. Praying is a direct communication with the creator of the Earth and the Heavens. It is a way to build a relationship with the Father. He listens to everything you say to Him and keeps all of your prayers for He is your friend. He will give you what you pray for if it aligns with His will for your life. In my prayers, I praise the Father for who He is, I thank the Father for what He has done, I ask the Father for forgiveness for what I have done and I ask the Father for what I need.

All these people, places, and things serve a purpose in my life, but nothing compares to the Bible. It is the collected works of God that reveal both His love and requirements for us and our privileges and responsibilities toward Him. The Bible has all of the answers you need, you have to read it.

God loves me so much, that He saw I was living my life the wrong way and wanted to fix it for my benefit. I idolized relationships, lived in fear, and was selfish, boastful, and prideful. I thought with the help of those self-help relationship books that I could make women fall and stay in love with me. I put all my happiness into relationships instead of with Christ. I was living this life by myself and wandered aimlessly in a life full of sin. I wouldn't let my dear savior in until I had no other choice. God fixed my ways on purpose because He loves me.

Thank you, Lord!

14

Jesus Is To Me

> *Ephesians 2:8-9*
>
> *"For it is by grace you have been saved, through faith—and this is not from yourselves, it is the gift of God—*
>
> *not by works, so that no one can boast."*

If I had to tell you one thing about Jesus it would be this, by grace through faith in Jesus Christ is your only way to heaven. Not by your works, but by faith in Jesus Christ and what he did for you on that cross, which is a gift from God. Jesus loves us so much, that He died on the cross for all of our sins, so through Him, we have a way to Heaven. That is where your salvation lives and it is the main topic of the New Testament in our Bibles. This is the Gospel that needs to be preached and everything else is a watered-down version. I have found other things with my pursuit of Christ, but that is not the main message of the Gospel.

Other things can come from your pursuit of Christ and what I have found Jesus to be; My peace, joy, hope, trust, forgiveness, future, salvation, and love.

> *Philippians 4:7*
>
> *"And the peace of God, which transcends all understanding, will guard your hearts and your minds in Christ Jesus."*

I have this peace about me that is hard to explain to others. I often tell people, "Jesus took my depression and anxieties away from me." They often look puzzled and questioned how Jesus could do that. I think we look at Jesus and put a limit on what we think He could do. If He was God, there is no limit to what Jesus could do for anyone, like taking my depression away. He is a God of miracles and I've learned never to limit Him in anything. When I saw the light, that is Christ, it came with peace. It is unexplainable to most because it doesn't seem possible.

> *James 1:2-3*
>
> *"Consider it pure joy, my brothers and sisters, whenever you face trials of many kinds,*
>
> *because you know that the testing of your faith produces perseverance."*

I have joy in this life now that I thought I would never get back. I went through a couple of heartbreaks which led me to live in fear. I was depressed because I was convinced that I would never find true love until I did. Jesus gives me joy because He has shown me time and time again how great He has been in my life. I reflect often on all the great things He has done for me in my life and it gives me pure joy to know that He loves me. I have been through my fair share of trials in life, which at the time brought me to a dark place, but now I wouldn't trade it for the world. That is how much joy I have in Christ.

Hebrews 6:11

"We want each of you to show this same diligence to the very end, so that what you hope for may be fully realized."

Jesus gave me hope in times of uncertainty. I don't personally see the future and how it will pan out, but I have hope that Jesus has already laid the path for me. I reflect on situations that I thought I wanted to happen in my life but would have turned out to be dreadful. He saved me from people, places, and things that I wanted because He knew it wasn't His purpose for my life. If you think you lost something that you can never replace it with, you would be surprised that He can replace it with something even better. You need to keep pursuing and have faith in Christ, wholeheartedly.

Proverbs 16:3

"Commit to the LORD whatever you do, and He will establish your plans."

I trust Christ with my life and everything in it. God and his grace are the reason why I have been born again in the Spirit and have been guided to the path I am now on. He has shown me numerous times how great He has been in directing my life to where it needs to go at precisely the perfect time. God's timing is perfect and transcends all understanding of human knowledge. I have been prideful and would complain to God about how I want this in my life, but when I look back, I understand why He didn't give it to me then. I was immature and wasn't ready for that blessing to be in my life. I trust the Lord and have committed to Him.

Colossians 3:13
"Bear with each other and forgive one another if any of you has a grievance against someone. Forgive as the Lord forgave you."

He is my forgiveness for He forgave me of all my sins. It took some time to forgive the girls that broke my heart because they brought me to the darkest time of my life. But I realize that I needed to be in the darkest time of my life to get to where I am now. I needed to become desperate so that I would grow. I was in a sink-or-swim situation and decided to swim. God had a plan for me and used them in it to get me to where I needed to go. I haven't spoken to them in years, but I have forgiven them as God has forgiven me. I also pray for their happiness and that they see Christ like I see Christ.

Philippians 1:6

"Being confident of this, that he who began a good work in you will carry it on to completion until the day of Christ Jesus."

My future is all tied to Jesus. He is the foundation of what my life is and will always be. I have prayed for wisdom, guidance, and discernment for my future and for Christ to be at the center of everything I do. I have no idea what the future holds, other than that Jesus is already preparing the way. In the past, I tried doing this life on my own and kept getting burnt. I didn't have much success and it eventually led me to rock bottom. From now on I give it all the Christ and I know He is already preparing the way.

John 14:6

"Jesus answered, "I am the way and the truth and the life. No one comes to the Father except through me."

Salvation by grace through faith in Jesus Christ is the main topic of the New Testament in our Bibles. Our salvation is all tied to having faith in Jesus Christ and what He did for us on that cross. You could be doing amazing things in this world for people, but you will still fall short of salvation. Your good works will not get you into Heaven because we have all sinned at least once in this life. That is why we are desperate for Jesus, our savior.

Matthew 6:33

"But seek first his kingdom and his righteousness, and all these things will be given to you as well."

Jesus is the love I have been searching for my entire life. The seeds of Christ have been planted throughout my life, but I still never pursued Him. He was always right there next to me and I never saw Him. I thought I would find love in a relationship with a woman, but I was humbled. I went to rock bottom and that is where I found Christ. He was there with me when I was at my lowest point. He has brought me peace, joy, hope, trust, forgiveness, future, salvation, and love. A relationship will bring a good thing into my life, but the source of my happiness is found in Christ and Christ alone.

Again, the main point of Jesus and the Gospel is, by grace through faith in Him is your only way to heaven. Not by your works, but by faith, which is a gift from God.

15

Nothing Is Happening

Proverbs 3:5-6

"Trust in the Lord with all your heart and lean not on your own understanding;

in all your ways submit to Him, and he will make your paths straight."

Since I have been pursuing Christ, you might think that my life has been virtuous. I have been living with peace, joy, and hope while my depression and anxieties have melted away. This is all true and I have found love in Christ, which is the ultimate love in this life, but it hasn't come without some complications.

I thought I would find a wife and a career quickly since I found Christ. I saw other Christians that were being blessed with all of this and some of these Christians were fresher in their pursuit of Christ than I was. I saw what non-believers had and was wondering why they had what I wanted. But, again, I was living with a joy that I have never experienced before.

I prayed multiple times, "Lord, I pray you to bring me to the girl you have planned for me to marry. I pray you bring us together, sooner rather than later. I also pray for a career where I can make a living and be able to support my family one day. In Jesus' name, Amen."

But nothing was happening in my life. My dating life was non-existent and the pursuit of a career was being shut down before I could even start. The dating pool seemed to dry up. I applied for numerous jobs and wouldn't get interviews. I was frustrated at the lack of progress that I thought I would have by now. "Christ is with me, no? How come other Christians and even non-believers are being blessed with what I want?" I would think to myself.

I figured I needed to get closer to God and get into the Bible more for Him to bless me. I kept pursuing Christ, turning away from temptations and I prayed all the time. I tried my absolute hardest to be perfect in everything I did and when I would mess up and sin, I would be miserable for the next couple of days. I thought that because I messed up and sinned, God wouldn't bless me with what I wanted. It was devastating.

I noticed that I often prayed for blessings rather than praying for guidance. Before when I was at rock bottom and had nowhere else to go, I prayed *"Show me where I need to go!"* I was asking for guidance and He gave it to me by bringing me to "The Right Fight" and again with the Bible. Instead of praying for a blessing, I decided to pray for guidance again since it has worked in the past.

I heard this prayer from a sermon I was watching online and it resonated with me enough that I prayed it. It was, "Lord will you search my heart and point out any evil ways in me." A couple of days later He would point out to me in a different sermon I was watching with Voddie Baucham. Voddie was straight to the point and talked about my situation of not getting what you have prayed for. For trying to be good, so God will bless you. Trying to read your Bible and praying, so that you can get what you want. It seems like the logical thing to do right? To glorify God in everything you do and then He would bless you with what you prayed for, right?

That is not the case at all. I was arrogant and God pointed it out to me. How prideful and arrogant I was thinking that God had to bless me because I pursued Him by reading my Bible and praying to Him throughout the day. I was being envious of other Christians because they were getting wives and careers that I thought I deserved too. I was pursuing Him to be blessed instead of pursuing Him to build a relationship with Him. I was sinning and didn't even know it. He isn't a genie. He searched my heart and pointed out the evil ways in me that I was being prideful, envious, and pursued Him for all the wrong reasons.

We live in an instant gratification generation with social media being at our fingertips. We want it all right in this instance without putting in the work and due diligence to succeed. Sure, God can give you want you have been praying for, but if you're not ready for it, lost in your pursuit of Him or it is not a part of His will for you, you won't get it. God loves us all and will bless us all with people, places, and things that He knows we need.

His timing is perfect and is above our understanding. I thought if I did this, God will bless me with this. My mentality was that if I don't sin, God will have to bless me, right? I was wrong and I'm grateful for Him pointing it out to me. He answered my prayer and taught me a valuable lesson.

Looking back, He has always been preparing me for something. I thought the something was a wife or a career, but I think that something was Him. He broke me down, to build me back up the way He wants me to be, to glorify Him in everything I do. To put Him first in my life and to not idolize people, places, and things above Him.

Every week I learn something valuable from God that I can take with me for the rest of my life. For example, I realized that I idolized being pure over Christ. You might ask, how can idolizing being pure be a bad thing? Sure, being pure is a great thing and something we should all strive for, but if you do it to get something from God then you are idolizing it over Him. The truth is, you're not going to be pure on your own, for Jesus purified us when His blood was shed on the cross. Our focus needs to be on Jesus and not on being pure. I needed to focus on Christ instead of trying to be pure because with Christ I am pure.

There could be many reasons why nothing is happening in my life. I could be living in a reoccurring sin that needs to be addressed or I haven't been prepared mentally, emotionally, spiritually, or physically for what is to come. There could be numerous reasons and the one that I keep coming back to is, testing my faith. God will test your faith to show you where you need to improve upon. I keep praying for, "When?" when it comes to the things I have prayed for.

Psalm 119:105
"Your word is a lamp for my feet, a light on my path."

Abraham has a similar story to mine. He reached the land that God promised for him and nothing was happening. He waited in faith for God's promises without seeing how or when it will happen and that strengthened his faith. Faith is waiting for God's promises without knowing the "when" or having explanations. God needed Abraham's faith to grow stronger until He blessed him with His promise.

God might not bless you because He wants you to build a relationship with Him. He doesn't want to be the genie in the bottle that grants every command that you give him. He wants you to seek Him and build a relationship with Him because He loves you. He might keep you alone because He wants you to pursue Him with all of your heart and not be distracted by this world and everything in it. If you have a family or are dating someone, your free time will be filled up with them. You might not have the time to pursue Christ and that is why I believe He doesn't answer our prayers all the time. He wants to have a relationship with you, trust me.

He has been guiding me to where I need to go, the people I need to meet, the videos I need to watch and the scripture I need to read. He knows what lies ahead and I trust Him entirely because I have seen what he has done in my life. I could get caught up on the "when," but in reality, I can't waste this time right now by doing nothing. I need to do what God wants me to do right now. Life gets busy and God has kept me alone and without a career because that is His plan for me right now. Maybe it is because I have more free time to pursue Him and also to prepare for what I need to be successful when He does bless me in the future. It is all about God's timing, for He knows best. I need to prepare myself for what God has in store for me because if I don't, I won't be able to fully enjoy the blessing He will bring to me.

I tend to let societal pressures get to me from time to time when it comes to dating or finding a career by a certain age, but in the end, I know God is number one in my life and that He has plans for me. If I conform to what this world wants of me, I'll end up rushing into a marriage or career that isn't right for me and I'll be miserable because of it. I've learned to trust God's timing in everything I do, pray about everything, and don't force anything. If it comes from God, it will come with peace.

God did miracles in the Bible and you might want a blessing in your life, I know I do. If that is what you are thinking, you are not alone. But you're missing the main point of Jesus. When Jesus fed five thousand people with only five loathes and two fish. It was a miracle that those people witnessed and would soon find themselves following Jesus. But, for the wrong reasons. Are you pursuing Christ because He can do miracles or are you pursuing Him for a relationship and eternal life? This was something that God pointed out to me when I prayed for Him *"to search my heart and point out any evil ways in me."*

John 6:26-27

"Jesus answered, "Very truly I tell you, you are looking for me, not because you saw the signs I performed but because you ate the loaves and had your fill.

Do not work for food that spoils, but for food that endures to eternal life, which the Son of Man will give you. For on him God the Father has placed his seal of approval."

16

To Live Is Christ

Revelation 3:15-16

"I know your deeds, that you are neither cold nor hot. I wish you were either one or the other!

So, because you are lukewarm—neither hot nor cold—I am about to spit you out of my mouth."

A man was sitting on a fence that divided a field into two parts. One part was Heaven with Christ and one part was hell with Satan. Christ and Satan both talked to the man pleading with him about what side of the fence he should come down on. The man listened to both intently, but couldn't make a decision. The man had no idea which side to go to. Finally, Christ and Satan left the man to be by himself and his thoughts.

Later on, Satan came back to the man on the fence and told him, "Oh I forgot somebody, there you are! Come with me!"

"No! I didn't choose Him and I definitely didn't choose you!" Said the man forcefully.

"The fence is mine," said Satan as he grabbed the man and dragged him to his side of the field.

The man's indecision to pick a side of the field was the ultimate deciding factor. Being a lukewarm Christian means that you have one foot in the world and the other foot with Christ. In Revelation 3:16 in the Bible, it says not to be lukewarm or He will be done with you. He doesn't have time for people that aren't going to commit to Him wholeheartedly. You can't love the things of this world and love Christ at the same time.

Philippians 1:21

"For to me, to live is Christ and to die is gain."

What is the first thing that comes to your mind when I say, "For to me, to live is Christ and to die is gain"? If we break it down into two separate parts, "to live is Christ" and "to die is gain," most people focus on the second part of the verse, "to die is gain." Which I think means as Christians that once we die, we gain and go to heaven. Heaven is more appealing than anything, right? How can it not be? The streets are paved with gold and there is a mansion for all of us. There will be peace, joy, and praise. God will wipe away all the tears away from your life that occurred on Earth. Heaven will be a majestic place and the best part, is that it will be our forever home.

Most people, unfortunately, forget about the first part of the verse, "to live is Christ." What exactly does that entail? I think it means to proclaim the gospel of Jesus Christ and to love as Jesus did. To live this life with the example of the way Christ lived his. To pursue His knowledge and learn about Him daily. Live with purpose and be obedient to God's word. What would Jesus do? That's what we want to do.

To live like Christ means giving up everything in your life that brings you further away from Him. Live with purpose and live like Christ. It will be an ongoing battle throughout your entire life and you will make mistakes, but it is worth it to dump this world and live like Christ. To bear the fruit of the spirit; love, joy, peace, patience, kindness, goodness, faithfulness, gentleness, and self-control. Being fruitful as often as you can because you never know who is watching you and your actions. God will use you in different ways throughout your life. Who knows, you might be the only Bible that someone reads, so act like it and bear the fruit of the spirit.

We all want to do vast and monumental things in this world that leaves a legacy. To impact this world positively and to be remembered by many. We want to be significant and leave an enormous impact. That is good and all, but recognize that sometimes vast and monumental things are different than we might think they are. God builds a legacy based on being faithful to the small things He gives us to do on a day-to-day basis. Being faithfully obedient on the agenda that He gives to us. For God knew what our day-to-day life was going to be before our bodies were even formed in our mother's womb.

Psalm 139:16
"Your eyes saw my unformed body;
all the days ordained for me were written in your book
before one of them came to be."

Everything you do should be for Christ. No matter the circumstances you should be glorifying God in everything you do. If you are in school, are you accomplishing the highest level you possibly can? Are the actions you are engaged in Christ-like? How are you treating your educators and school staff? Do your friends and colleagues know that you are a Christian? You never know how God will use you. Again, you might be the only Bible someone ever reads one day, so you better try to act like it.

Many nonbelievers think that being a Christian means you're supposed to act a certain way and that Christians are hypocrites. I agree that as Christians should act a certain way and that we are all hypocrites, but it is not for the same reasons as what nonbelievers state. A nonbeliever says that as a Christian you should never sin and live a life as pure as God wants you to. As a Christian, I know that this is not possible and that is why Jesus Christ dying for our sins makes us pure. Nothing that we do on earth will make us pure or will get us into heaven and that is why we are desperate for Christ because He, alone, makes us pure. We may be hypocrites, but the truth is that we are only pure through Christ.

To have your mind transformed by God and his word. To pray continually without ceasing. To love your neighbor as yourself. To not worry about tomorrow, for tomorrow will worry about itself. To bear the fruit of the spirit. To pursue righteousness, godliness, faith, love, endurance, and gentleness. To live in Christ and to die is gain.

17

Are You Truly Happy

Romans 10:9

"If you declare with your mouth, "Jesus is Lord,"
and believe in your heart that God raised Him
from the dead, you will be saved."

If I had to ask you one question about your life it would be, are you truly happy?

I thought I was before I met Christ, but the truth is I was miserable. I was chasing love and trying to find the one to complete me. I was let down many times and it eventually led to depression. I was filled with anxiety and lived in fear that I would never find love. I think I have had a great life, but something was always missing from it and I always thought it was a wife.

When I met Christ, it was then that everything started to make sense. He was the missing piece that I was searching for my whole life. I had pure joy that I haven't felt since I was a child and my depression would eventually melt away. It was supernatural and is hard to explain, but with Christ, He gives you joy and hope. My happiness lives with Christ now and the blessings I have received are the icing on top of the cake.

But it is not about the blessings. In fact, it is about the gospel of Jesus Christ and the spiritual aspect of it. What He did on the cross for all of us sinners, so that through faith in Him we get to heaven. He is my foundation now and I put Him first in everything I do.

Everyone that has seen the light that is Jesus Christ has their own story about how it happened. For me, Christ was planted into my life at a young age by my parents bringing me to Church and praying before every meal we had as a family. Then, throughout my life, the seeds were watered by people, places, and things God brought into my life. He tried to get my attention and it took me until I was twenty-eight years old for me to blossom and see the light that is Christ. I had to go to rock bottom where I would become desperate and had nowhere to go, but up.

God called on me several times in my life, but I chose to ignore his call. I could have seen the light earlier in my life, but instead, God had to bring me to rock bottom to get my attention where I would become desperate. That might seem harsh to you, but He did it out of love. I needed to change my life because I was going down the wrong path which was filled with depression, anxiety, and fear. He corrected me just like my parents corrected me growing up. It is what someone would do to someone they love. I was just too stubborn and prideful to see Christ earlier.

He went through the most painful death invented by man. To be crucified is a slow and painful death where He was nailed to the cross through His hands and feet which was painful, but on top of that, He was bearing the weight of all of our sins. To breathe out, He had to push down on the nails in His feet to raise His body, and allow His rib cage to move downwards and inwards to expire air from His lungs. The movements were excruciating on his wrists, shoulders, chest, and legs and the muscle tissue would all begin to separate. He was on that cross for roughly six hours while being covered in blood and sweat. Painful is an understatement.

Christ loves us more than anyone or anything else can or will on this earth. He was thinking of you when He died on that cross for your sins so that through Him you can get to heaven. He paid the price on that cross for you because He loves you.

It doesn't matter how many times you have sinned in your life; Christ will accept you. Some might think that they have done some terrible things in the past and that God doesn't love them, but the truth is, that He does and will always love you. We are all sinners and there is no difference between the preacher and you. The heavens will shout with joy every time a sinner confesses his sins and repents. It is never too late to accept Jesus.

If you want to pursue Christ and don't know where to start, I would confess my sins and declare Jesus Christ as your Lord and Savior. Then, I would start by reading your Bible. When my boss, Steve, told me to read the Bible, he told me to start with "John" and to use the New International Version. It is a more accessible version to read than most others. I would personally start reading at the beginning of the New Testament with "Matthew" and continue reading to the end of the Bible. This way you start with the four Gospels, Matthew, Mark, Luke, and John, and you will understand who and what Jesus did when He was here with us.

A YouTube channel, "Bible Project" has videos on each book in the Bible and gives you a better understanding of what is going on. I would watch a video on "Matthew" and then go ahead with reading the book of "Matthew." It helped me out tremendously because there are a lot of characters, events, and confusing parts involved in each book. It simplified the Bible for me and made it not seem overwhelming.

Praying is an essential part of being a Christian. It is your only way to directly talk to the creator of the earth and the heavens. Ask God in prayer for guidance, wisdom, and discernment for He will help you.

Jesus wants a relationship with you. He was thinking about you when He was on that cross. Go and accept Him before it is too late. For He loves you more than you could even fathom. It is incomprehensible to our human knowledge, but trust me, He is worth pursuing with all of your heart.

John 3:16

"For God so loved the world that He gave his one and only Son, that whoever believes in Him shall not perish but have eternal life."

ACKNOWLEDGMENTS

Thank you, Mom and Dad, for giving me more than I could ask for. Because of your love for Me, Katelynn, and Connor, I grew up knowing what it takes to love someone with all of your heart. I learned that a parent's love for their children is just like God's love for His. Love gives and protects forever.

Thank you, Mom and Dad, for bringing Christ into my life at an early age. We went to Church, celebrated Easter and Christmas, and prayed before every meal. Looking back, these things had an enormous effect and were the seeds of Christ that were planted into my life. Without this, I would be lost today.

Thank you, and I love you.

SCRIPTURE REFERENCES

"Access Your Bible from Anywhere." BibleGateway.com: A Searchable Online Bible in over 150 Versions and 50 Languages., https://www.biblegateway.com/. (New International Version)

The Scriptures are in chronological order that they were used in this book.

Psalm 18:16

"He reached down from Heaven and Rescued me; he drew me out of deep waters."

Isaiah 41:10

"So do not fear, for I am with you; do not be dismayed, for I am your God. I will strengthen you and help you; I will uphold you with my righteous right hand."

John 15:13

"Greater love has no one than this: to lay down one's life for one's friends."

Proverbs 18:22

"He who finds a wife finds what is good and receives favor from the Lord."

1 Corinthians 13:13

"And now these three remain: faith, hope and love. But the greatest of these is love."

Psalm 34:18

"The Lord is close to the brokenhearted and saves those who are crushed in spirit."

Jeremiah 29:11

"For I know the plans I have for you," declares the Lord, "plans to prosper you and not to harm you, plans to give you hope and a future."

1 Peter 5:7

"Cast all your anxiety on Him because He cares for you."

Proverbs 16:4

"The LORD works out everything to its proper end— even the wicked for a day of disaster."

Ecclesiastes 3:1

"There is a time for everything, and a season for every activity under the heavens"

Ephesians 4:2

"Be completely humble and gentle; be patient, bearing with one another in love."

2 Corinthians 12:9

"But he said to me, "My grace is sufficient for you, for my power is made perfect in weakness."

Therefore, I will boast all the more gladly about my weaknesses, so that Christ's power may rest on me."

2 Corinthians 5:20

"We are therefore Christ's ambassadors, as though God were making his appeal through us. We implore you on Christ's behalf: Be reconciled to God."

John 3:3

"Jesus replied, "Very truly I tell you, no one can see the kingdom of God unless they are born again."

Galatians 5:22-23

"But the fruit of the Spirit is love, joy, peace, patience, kindness, goodness, faithfulness, gentleness,

self-control; against such things there is no law."

Mark 11:24

"Therefore, I tell you, whatever you ask for in prayer, believe that you have received it, and it will be yours."

Isaiah 41:10

"So do not fear, for I am with you; do not be dismayed, for I am your God.

I will strengthen you and help you; I will uphold you with my righteous right hand."

Isaiah 48:10

"See, I have refined you, though not as silver; I have tested you in the furnace of affliction."

Ephesians 2:8-9

"For it is by grace you have been saved, through faith—and this is not from yourselves, it is the gift of God—

not by works, so that no one can boast."

Philippians 4:7

"And the peace of God, which transcends all understanding, will guard your hearts and your minds in Christ Jesus."

James 1:2-3

"Consider it pure joy, my brothers and sisters, whenever you face trials of many kinds,

because you know that the testing of your faith produces perseverance."

Hebrews 6:11

"We want each of you to show this same diligence to the very end, so that what you hope for may be fully realized."

Proverbs 16:3

"Commit to the LORD whatever you do, and he will establish your plans."

Colossians 3:13

"Bear with each other and forgive one another if any of you has a grievance against someone.

Forgive as the Lord forgave you."

Philippians 1:6

"Being confident of this, that he who began a good work in you will carry it on to completion until the day of Christ Jesus."

John 14:6

"Jesus answered, "I am the way and the truth and the life. No one comes to the Father except through me."

Matthew 6:33

"But seek first his kingdom and his righteousness, and all these things will be given to you as well."

Proverbs 3:5-6

"Trust in the Lord with all your heart and lean not on your own understanding;

in all your ways submit to Him, and he will make your paths straight."

Psalm 119:105

"Your word is a lamp for my feet, a light on my path."

John 6:26-27

"Jesus answered, "Very truly I tell you, you are looking for me, not because you saw the signs I performed

but because you ate the loaves and had your fill.

Do not work for food that spoils, but for food that endures to eternal life, which the Son of Man will give you.

For on Him God the Father has placed his seal of approval."

Revelation 3:15-16

"I know your deeds, that you are neither cold nor hot. I wish you were either one or the other!

So, because you are lukewarm—neither hot nor cold—I am about to spit you out of my mouth."

Philippians 1:21

"For to me, to live is Christ and to die is gain."

Psalm 139:16

"Your eyes saw my unformed body;

all the days ordained for me were written in your book

before one of them came to be."

Romans 10:9

"If you declare with your mouth, "Jesus is Lord," and believe in your heart that God raised Him from the dead, you will be saved."

John 3:16

"For God so loved the world that He gave his one and only Son, that whoever believes in Him shall not perish but have eternal life."

Colossians 1:9

"For this reason, since the day we heard about you, we have not stopped praying for you.

We continually ask God to fill you with the knowledge of his will through all the wisdom and understanding that the Spirit gives"

ABOUT THE AUTHOR

The author, Tyler Matthew Gebhardt, was born in 1992 in Denver, Colorado. He got his Bachelor of Arts degree at Metropolitan State University of Denver in 2017. He is a published author and a devoted follower of Christ. He wants everyone to see Him as he sees Him. The purpose of this book was to lead you in the direction of Christ and not as a substitute for the Bible.

If you have any questions or comments about this book or anything Christ-related. Feel free to reach out to him on Social Media *@tylermatthewgebhardt* and/or Email at *tylermatthewgebhardt@gmail.com*

@tylermatthewgebhardt

tylermatthewgebhardt@gmail.com

My prayer is that this book helps you understand who God really is. I hope, from these pages, you can understand better what true love is. May these pages bring you closer to Jesus and show you why we need Him in our lives.

In Jesus' name, Amen.

Colossians 1:9

"For this reason, since the day we heard about you, we have not stopped praying for you. We continually ask God to fill you with the knowledge of his will through all the wisdom and understanding that the Spirit gives"

*This book is not a substitution for the Bible. The purpose of this book was to lead you in that direction.

www.ingramcontent.com/pod-product-compliance
Lightning Source LLC
Chambersburg PA
CBHW070726130626
46553CB00005B/2169